Word Formation in
Generative Grammar

Linguistic Inquiry Monographs
Samuel Jay Keyser, general editor

1. *Word Formation in Generative Grammar*
   Mark Aronoff
2. *$\bar{X}$ Syntax: A Study of Phrase Structure*
   Ray Jackendoff
3. *Recent Transformational Studies in European Languages*
   Samuel Jay Keyser, editor
4. *Studies in Abstract Phonology*
   Edmund Gussmann
5. *An Encyclopedia of AUX: A Study in Cross-Linguistic Equivalence*
   Susan Steele

Word Formation in
Generative Grammar

Mark Aronoff

The MIT Press, Cambridge, Massachusetts, and London, England

Second printing, 1981

© 1976 by Massachusetts Institute of Technology

All rights reserved. No part of this book may be reproduced in any form or by any means, electronic or mechanical, including photocopying, recording, or by any information storage and retrieval system, without permission in writing from the publishers.

ISBN 0-262-51017-0

Printed and bound in the United States of America

Contents

Foreword	ix
Preface	xi
1. Ground	1
1.1. Derivation and Inflection	2
1.2. Other Types of Morphology	3
1.3. A Brief Survey of the Recent History of the Study of Morphology	4
1.4. The Return of Morphology	5
2. Teleology	7
2.1. Trouble with Morphemes	7
2.1.1. Minimal Signs	8
2.1.2. Words	8
2.1.3. Morphemes	10
2.1.3.1. Cranberry Morphs	10
2.1.3.2. Other Berries	10
2.1.3.3. Prefix=Stem (latinate)	11
2.1.3.4. A Similar Class	14
2.1.3.5. Defining the Morpheme	15
2.1.4. Trouble with Words?	15
2.1.4.1. Cranberry Words	15
2.1.4.2. The Numerous Verbs *Stand*	16
2.1.5. A Historical Note on Inflection	17
2.2. Word Formation	17
2.2.1. Possible and Actual Words	17
2.2.2. Types of New Words	19
2.2.3. What Are New Words Coined From?	20
2.2.3.1. Oddities	20
2.2.3.2. Words from Morphemes	21
2.2.3.3. Word-based Morphology	21
2.2.3.4. Word Formation Rules	22
2.2.3.5. Assumptions about the Lexicon	22

2.2.4. Evidence for the Proposal	23
2.2.4.1. The Phonological Cycle	23
2.2.4.2. Irregular Back-formations	27
2.2.5. Counterevidence	28
2.2.6. Word Structure	30
3. Productivity	**35**
3.1. Preliminaries	35
3.2. #*ness* and +*ity*	37
3.2.1. Semantics	38
3.2.2. Phonology	40
3.2.3. Lexical Government and the Lexicon	43
3.3. Conclusions	45
4. Word Formation Rules	**46**
4.1. Syntax and Semantics	47
4.1.1. The Base and the Unitary Base Hypothesis	47
4.1.2. The Output	49
4.2. Morphology	51
4.2.1. Morphological Restrictions on the Base	51
4.2.1.1. Abstract Morphological Features	51
4.2.1.2. Restrictions Statable on Individual Morphemes	53
4.2.2. Encoding Morphological Restrictions	55
4.2.2.1. Ordering of WFRs	56
4.2.2.2. Unordered WFRs	61
4.3. Phonology	63
4.3.1. The Phonological Operation	63
4.3.1.1. Copying Rules	64
4.3.1.2. Infixing	69
4.3.1.3. Consequences	70
4.3.2. The Place of the Phonological Operation in the Grammar	72
4.3.2.1. Reduplication Paradoxes	73
4.3.2.2. Deletions	78
4.3.2.3. Boundaries and Phonological Conditions	79
4.3.2.4. Implications	80
4.3.3. Boundaries and Cycles	81
4.3.4. Problems	82
4.3.4.1. A Condition on the Surface Form of the Output	82
4.3.4.2. A Global Phonological Condition	82
4.3.4.3. A Transderivational Constraint	83
4.3.4.4. A Boundary Paradox	84
4.4. Summary	85

5. Adjustment Rules	87
5.1. The Place and Role of Adjustment	87
5.2. Truncation Rules	88
5.2.1. +*ee*	88
5.2.2. +*ant*	90
5.2.3. Comparative +*er*	92
5.2.4. TruncaWFRs	94
5.2.5. Truncation and Phonology	94
5.2.6. Russian Truncation	95
5.2.7. German *ge-* Deletion	97
5.3. Allomorphy Rules	98
5.3.1. *ion*	99
5.3.1.1. Allomorphs of +*Ation*	100
5.3.1.2. +*Ation*	100
5.3.1.3. Stems of the Form *X+ate*	101
5.3.1.4. The Marked Roots	102
5.3.2. Root Allomorphy	105
5.3.2.1. *fy* and *ply*	110
5.3.3. Other Allomorphy	111
5.3.4. Allomorphy and Other Parts of a Grammar	112
6. Exempla	115
6.1. Distributional Arguments	115
6.2. *-able*	121
6.2.1. Phonological Arguments	122
6.2.1.1. Stress	122
6.2.1.2. Allomorphy	123
6.2.1.3. Truncation	124
6.2.1.4. Summary	125
6.2.2. Correlates	125
6.2.2.1. Morphological Correlates	125
6.2.2.2. Syntactic Correlates	126
6.2.2.3. Semantic Correlates	127
6.2.3. Summary	128
References	130

Foreword

We are pleased to present this monograph as the first in the series *Linguistic Inquiry Monographs*. These monographs will present new and original research beyond the scope of the article. Because of their originality it is hoped that they will benefit our field by bringing to it perspectives that will stimulate further research and insight.

Samuel Jay Keyser

Preface

What follows represents an attempt to integrate what I believe to be a reasonably well-motivated account of morphological structure into a general theory of generative grammar. The work deals mainly with questions of derivational morphology, though inflection is touched upon briefly in a few places; compounds, despite the title, will not be discussed.

Historically, morphology and generative grammar have been uneasy bedfellows, and I cannot presume that all of my readers will be equally conversant with both. On morphology, happily, there are several good introductory works. The relevant sections of Bloomfield (1933) are, to my mind, the best of these. Matthews (1974) is more detailed and also contains discussions of many of the more persistent problems. These problems have also received great attention in the structuralist literature on morphemic analysis. Bloch (1947), Hockett (1947), Nida (1948), and Harris (1948) form the classic core. Harris' views are presented in further detail in his *Methods* book (1951). As for generative grammar, I adopt the general perspective of Chomsky (1972a) and Chomsky and Halle (1968) (henceforth SPE).

A few words about personal peculiarities. In the tradition of SPE, I tend to use spelling where others might use transcription. I will only use transcription when I wish to emphasize phonological properties. In these cases I use square brackets ([ ]) not solely for phonetic transcription but, as in SPE, indiscriminately to represent any level of a phonological derivation. I depart from this practice only when quoting from other sources. I have avoided the term *lexeme* for personal reasons and use instead the term *word*. This means that I have no way of distinguishing an uninflected word (lexeme) from an inflected word (word). I am confident that the ambiguity will not cause much grief. I use the term *morpheme* in the American structuralist sense, which means that a morpheme must have phonological substance and cannot be simply a unit of meaning. Entities such as PLURAL and PAST, which have many phonological realizations and which were problematic within earlier frameworks, are considered to be syntactic markers and not morphemes.

We find comfort in precedent. It is convenient when introducing a notion which may not be uncontroversial to defend the introduction with an allusion to its commonness in older thought. This may reflect a deep ecclesiastian conviction. It is more conventionally considered to be a sign of modesty. Modesty, though, is a convenient cover for a less virtuous attitude: when something is not ours, we can easily disclaim ultimate responsibility for it. With this in mind, let me say that the basic view of the workings of morphology presented in this work is not new.

However, to my knowledge, there has been no previous attempt to integrate it into the general framework which I am proposing, that of generative transformational grammar. I believe that this framework is essentially correct. The truth or falsity of my views must be proved within it, not within some more general theory of epistemology, and all responsibility for the assertion of these views therefore rests with me. Nevertheless, I must acknowledge my precedessors and others who have helped to form my thoughts, and my debts to them.

I have benefited greatly from the work of Hans Marchand, especially his book *The Categories and Types of Present-Day English Word-Formation* (1969). Marchand's views on the workings of word structure are a principal source of mine, though the framework in which he is working is radically different. The book has also been a valuable source of data. There is no more complete work on the subject of English morphology. Of the small literature on morphology within generative grammar I owe much to Karl Zimmer's *Affixal Negation* (1964), Morris Halle's "Prolegomena to a Theory of Word-Formation" (1973a), Uriel Weinreich's "Problems in the Analysis of Idioms" (1969), and Dorothy Siegel's regrettably still unpublished "Some Lexical Transderivational Constraints in English" (1971).

The sketch of English phonology presented in SPE has been as indispensable as it must be to any work remotely connected with that domain. The influence of Paul Kiparsky's "Phonological Representations" (1973) has also been considerable. In syntax, I have adopted the lexicalist hypothesis of Chomsky's "Remarks on Nominalization" (1970). This monograph, however, does not depend on the extended standard theory of Chomsky (1972b, 1973), though my own prejudices towards that viewpoint are undeniable. On the most general plane I must cite two works, Noam Chomsky's *Aspects of the Theory of Syntax* (1965) and Ludwig Wittgenstein's *Philosophical Investigations* (1953), which I can only hope not to have abused.

This work is a somewhat revised and expanded version of my 1974 MIT doctoral dissertation. I am especially indebted to Morris Halle, my thesis director and esteemed colleague, for discussion throughout and since the preparation of that document. I am similarly grateful to Ken Hale and Paul Kiparsky, the other members of my thesis committee, and to my fellow students Alan Prince, Richard Oehrle, John Ross, Dorothy Siegel, and Edwin Williams. Frank Anshen, Emmon Bach, Alice Davison, and Steve Lapointe have provided invaluable comments on the earlier version. Frances Kelley has guided me through much of the revision.

The research of which this monograph is a result was made possible by doctoral fellowships from the Canada Council and the Department of Education of the Province of Quebec. I am grateful to these bodies.

Mark Aronoff
June 1975
Sound Beach and Old Field, New York

Word Formation in
Generative Grammar

1: Ground

We will be concerned in this work with the internal structure of words, a subject which, in the linguistic literature, is called *morphology*.

The notion *word* has long concerned students of language. Its definition is a long-standing problem in linguistics, and entire volumes have been devoted to the subject (e.g. Worth (1972)). A reasonably detailed procedure for isolating phonological words (units which may be considered as words for phonological purposes) is provided in Chomsky and Halle (1968, 366-370; henceforth SPE). Further refinements of this approach are discussed in Selkirk (1972). Syntactically, Postal (1969) puts forth a persuasive argument that the word, as a syntactic unit, corresponds to the *anaphoric island*, which is a syntactic string the internal elements of which cannot participate in anaphora. Though semantic definition of the notion is a traditional goal, it has not, to my knowledge, been achieved.

To say that morphology is word structure is not to say that all of the structure of the word is encompassed in the domain of morphology. There is a branch of phonology, termed *phonotactics* or *morpheme structure*, which concerns itself with the determination of possible sequences of sounds in a given language, "possible phonetic words". This is not morphology. Morphology treats words as *signs*: that is, not just as forms, but as meaningful forms. It is therefore concerned with words which are not simple signs, but which are made up of more elementary ones. This concern encompasses two distinct but related matters: first, the analysis of existing composite words, and second, the formation of new composite words. A unified theory of morphology should be capable of dealing with both of these areas in a unified and coherent manner, though it may not be possible or even desirable, as we will argue below, to treat them in exactly the same manner.

On the subject of unified theories, it should be stressed that morphology, as defined, is a small subsystem of the entire system of a language. A theory of morphology must be integrated or at least integrable into a fairly specific general theory of language. As a subsystem and a subtheory, morphology may have its own peculiarities; a system can be unified without being completely uniform. However, it does not exist in a vacuum. The present work is conceived in the general framework of transformational grammar as outlined in such works as Chomsky (1965) and SPE. More particularly, it presupposes the lexicalist hypothesis of Chomsky (1970) and at least the spirit, if not the letter, of Kiparsky's views with regard to phonological abstractness, discussed in Kiparsky (1973).

1.1. Derivation and Inflection

There are traditionally two types of morphological phenomena, *derivational* and *inflectional*. The distinction is delicate, and sometimes elusive, but nonetheless important. Inflection is generally viewed as encompassing the "purely grammatical" markers, those for tense, aspect, person, number, gender, case, etc. Within a lexicalist theory of syntax (cf. Chomsky (1970)), inflectional morphemes would be dominated by the node X, and perhaps higher nodes (cf. Siegel (1974)), while derivational morphemes would be dominated by the node X. Derivational morphology is thus restricted to the domain of *lexical category*.

It is generally true, and in accord with the lexicalist formalism, that derivational markers will be encompassed within inflectional markers. In the English word *compart+ment+al#ize#d*, for example, the last morpheme, *#d*, is inflectional, and all those internal to it are derivational. The two sets may not be interspersed. Thus the word *compart+ment+al#iz+ation#s* is possible, though the word **compart+ment+al#ize#d+ation#s* is not.

One peculiarity of inflection is that it is *paradigmatic*. Thus, every English nonmodal verb exhibits a paradigm consisting of the following forms:

    V   V#s   V#d_1 V#d_2 V#ing

For example:

    sigh   sighs   sighed   (has) sighed   sighing
    go   goes   went   (has) gone   going

The verb *go* exhibits *suppletion*, the filling of one of the slots of the paradigm by a phonologically unrelated form. Since derivational morphology is not paradigmatic, it does not show any suppletion: that is, it does not concern itself with phonologically dissimilar but semantically related forms.

Sometimes a paradigm is *defective*, lacking a form. The missing form is almost always the uninflected one. So, in English, we have *scissors*, *pants*, and *trousers*, but not **scissor*, **pant*, or **trouser*, except, of course, in derived forms, where (as the following examples demonstrate) the constraint on the mixing of morphologies still holds:

    scissorlike   *scissorslike
    trouserleg   *trousersleg[1]

A fuller description of some of the properties of inflectional morphology can be found in Bloomfield (1933). An independent characterization of the properties of derivational morphology is more difficult. Nida (1949) suggests the following: if, in a syntactic class (defined by substitution in his system, and in corresponding ways in other theories), we find items which are monomorphemic, then the polymorphemic items in that class are derived by the system of derivational morphology. The most immediate problem for such a definition is the existence of suppletive forms, such as *went* above, which, by Nida's criterion, would force us to include the past tense suffix in derivational rather than inflectional morphology. This is where the paradigm enters. We find that the past tense is a paradigmatic category, and therefore must be

---

[1] The behavior of *pants* is exceptional:
    pantspocket   *pantpocket
    pantsleg   *pantleg

inflectional. We might also invoke more abstract syntactic evidence to show that though *went* is monomorphemic on the surface, there is evidence for an abstract past tense morpheme. This is more difficult, though perhaps possible. In any case, as he himself notes, Nida's simple criterion must be amended to exclude clearly suppletive forms which are members of paradigms.[2]

1.2. Other Types of Morphology

Derivation and inflection do not exhaust the domain of morphology. There are "grammatical" morphological phenomena which cannot be subsumed under inflection. The best known of these is that of incorporation or cliticization. In Classical Hebrew, for example, under specific conditions (basically, when they are anaphoric rather than deictic) definite pronominal objects are incorporated into the verb, forming a single phonological unit with it. There is no question here of inflection, since this specific form of the verb only occurs when we would otherwise expect a definite pronoun object. A similar situation holds in English (cf. Selkirk (1972)).

A slightly more complicated example along the same lines comes from Syriac. Here, in addition to pronoun object cliticization, we have the copying of a pronoun for any definite object, other than anaphoric pronouns. The copied pronoun is cliticized to the verb, giving the same verb form as that containing the pronoun object. Clearly, the copying and the cliticization are both syntactic facts, and they are not paradigmatic.

Sometimes other material than pronouns can be incorporated into the verb. In Navaho, a specific adverb may sometimes occur inside the verb, and sometimes elsewhere in the sentence, but never in both places in the same sentence. This fact can be most easily captured by a syntactic movement rule.

---

[2] More difficult for Nida are cases of syntactically or semantically arbitrary forms. Consider, for example, the noun *police* in the following example:

(i) The police have arrested six people already.

The verb shows us that the noun is syntactically plural. Unlike a word like *sheep*, which is ambiguous between singular and plural, *police*, in this sense at least, never appears in a singular context. Here, we cannot argue in any straightforward way for the existence of a zero plural marker, as in *sheep*. Nor can a paradigm help, since there is none. In fact, a noun like *police* is disturbingly similar to the sort of item which Nida would invoke to show that one is dealing with a derivational system. Consider the set of agentive occupational nouns shown below.

	a.	b.	c.
(ii)	baker	cook	chef
	packer	pilot	chauffeur
	painter	coach	smith
	hunter		mechanic
	tanner		surgeon

The items in column (a) exhibit a suffix: *-er*; those in (b) might be derived by zero derivation from the corresponding verb. The items in (c), however, have no corresponding verb from which they may be derived. This is exactly the type of example Nida uses to show that a class like that of agentive occupational nouns is not inflectional. But is not *police* like the items in (c)? Ideally, we would like to have a syntactic theory which allows a zero morpheme in *police* (plural) but not in *chef*. We do not yet have such a theory. In any case, Nida's simple criterion is not sufficient to capture our intuitive notion of what exactly is meant by *derivational category*.

There is no traditional term for this third type of morphology. It is clearly "syntactic", and on that ground it can be grouped together with inflection, as opposed to derivation. There is often a clear historical connection between pronoun copying and cliticization and verbal agreement, and it may very well be that all agreement arises by a falling away from and generalization of pronoun cliticization. This would of course strengthen the contention that this third type of morphological phenomenon and inflection are really of the same nature, and opposed to derivation.

I will accept this opposition in the greater part of the body of this work and restrict the scope of further discussion to the domain of derivational morphology. This restriction will be relaxed only in regard to the interaction of phonology and morphology, where morphology encompasses both inflectional and derivational markers.

1.3. A Brief Survey of the Recent History of the Study of Morphology

Morphology is not something new or, like syntax, something much talked about for many years but little studied or understood. The early Indo-Europeanists, Bopp for instance, were interested almost solely in morphology, and morphology has remained one of the mainstays of the philological tradition (cf. the extensive bibliography in Marchand (1969)). Though their tools were better adapted to phonological and morphophonemic purposes, American descriptivists did do much substantive work in the area of morphology as we have defined it.

In the specific area of English morphology, I have already cited Marchand (1969) and my debt to it. Jespersen also devoted a volume of his *Modern English Grammar* to the subject. Among more recent works, I will note Zimmer's monograph on affixal negation (1964), which is notable for its concern with semantics and the very general and difficult problem of productivity.

Within the generative framework, morphology was for a long time quite successfully ignored. There was a good ideological reason for this: in its zeal, post-*Syntactic Structures* linguistics saw phonology and syntax everywhere, with the result that morphology was lost somewhere in between. For proponents of early generative grammar, grammar consisted of syntax and phonology. Phonology, at last freed from its phonemic blinkers, encompassed all of morphophonemics and phonemics in a grand system of ordered rules. Syntax took care of everything else: "all of the grammatical sequences of morphemes of a language" (Chomsky (1957, 32)). Within such a framework, morphology is not a separate study. In fact, though some of the earliest studies in transformational syntax were specifically restricted to the domain of the word (e.g. Lees (1960)), this domain was not considered to differ in any real way from that of the sentence. Even very recently, the school of generative semantics has insisted that the word is fundamentally no different from any other syntactic unit, tnus espousing a position like that of early generative grammar, which in essence denies the independence of morphology.

Recently, a substantial interest has arisen in the peculiarities of inflection as a separable syntactic phenomenon. The first study in this area was that of Bierwisch (1967). It has been followed by others, of which I will note Wurzel (1970) and Kiefer (1970, 1973). I will not discuss these works here, as their research lies outside the domain established for this monograph.

1.4. The Return of Morphology

Morphology found its way back into generative linguistics through several rear doors, almost simultaneously. The first hints that there might be something between syntax and phonology are found in SPE. There the question is first raised of whether the output of the syntactic component is in fact the input to the phonological component. It is noted that there are "certain discrepancies", and that "... the grammar must contain certain rules converting the surface structures generated by the syntactic component into a form appropriate for use by the phonological component." The rules referred to in this passage divide surface structure into phonological phrases. They are called *readjustment rules* and are supposed generally to "involve elimination of structure". An illuminating discussion of such rules is contained in Selkirk (1972). But these are not the only rules called readjustment rules. There are in addition rules which "eliminate grammatical formatives in favor of phonological matrices", for example converting $[[\text{sing}]_V \text{past}]_V$ into *sung* and $[[\text{mend}]_V \text{past}]_V$ into *mended*. The term *readjustment rule* is obviously being used broadly, for these last rules are clearly rules of inflectional morphology. Yet a third type of readjustment rule is in no way connected with elimination of structure. This sort applies (SPE, 223)

> ... to specific derivable formatives; for example the rule (110):

$$(110) \quad t \to d / = \begin{Bmatrix} \text{mi} \underline{} + \text{ive} \\ \text{ver} \underline{} + \text{ion} \end{Bmatrix}$$

Rule (110) is a very different sort of morphological rule. It is a rule of allomorphy, which spells out the form of particular morphemes in specific morphological environments.

We see, then, in SPE, the beginnings of a recognition of the independence of certain classes of phenomena from syntax and phonology. The term *readjustment rule* is not a particularly well-defined one, but among the rules so termed we do find a significant number which are plainly morphological.

SPE inadvertently created in its wake a second entrance for morphology. The purely formal spirit of Chomsky's and Halle's approach to phonology in general, and of the sketch of English phonology presented in SPE in particular, prompted a reaction. It was felt by many scholars, most prominently Kiparsky, that by disregarding concrete evaluation measures Chomsky and Halle were often led to propose phonological systems which were too abstract and to abuse the classificatory function of the phonetic features. Historically, these criticisms can be seen as a reaction to the excesses of revolutionary fervor. Remember that Chomsky and Halle were fighting against a theory which termed phonological only the most apparent of alternations and which put all others into one morphophonemic bag of lists, without regard for the differences in regularity among them. The revolutionary step of these pioneers was to pull down the phonemic barrier and declare all alternations to be the province of phonology. But, said their critics, surely not all connections are phonologically regular? Most of those which were earlier included under the morphophonemic label can indeed be treated as phonologically governed rules, but there is some limit. There are alternations which are just not determined by purely phonological features.

A further step, one which the critics have by and large not taken, is to ask whether some of these alternations which are not phonologically determined are in fact not part of the phonology at all. I will argue below that a class of rules which a more tightly constrained theory rejects as not optimal phonological rules can be fruitfully included in a theory of morphology.

Thus, because of a desire to place restrictions on the power of phonological theory, we find that certain phenomena now lie outside the domain of the theory. Many of these phenomena can be seen as morphological. We find the same kind of pattern that came to light in SPE.

A similar retreat took place at about the same time in syntax. In an attempt to restrict the power of grammatical theory, certain phenomena were removed from the domain of the syntax. In contrast with phonology, however, where the realization that the system as it stood could not be sufficiently constrained came gradually and inexorably, with very little objection on anyone's part to at least the spirit of the trend and with curiously few suggestions as to the nature of the discarded material or what should be done with it, morphology sprang out of syntax's thigh full-blown and caused a great to-do when it did so. The birth of morphology, or at least the declaration of its domain, is simultaneous with, and contained in, Chomsky's "Remarks on Nominalization" (1970). This paper presents a new theory of syntax, in which all of derivational morphology is isolated and removed from the syntax; it is instead dealt with in an expanded lexicon, by a separate component of the grammar. This distinction legitimizes the field of morphology as an independent entity.

"Remarks on Nominalization" was long and bitterly opposed, mainly, I believe, on esthetic grounds. Where previous and rival theories view language as one vast domain, encompassed by pervasive constraints (cf. Postal (1972)), Chomsky prefers to see language as divided into smaller well-distinguished units, each governed by its own, perhaps idiosyncratic, rules. As the reader will discover, I am more inclined toward the latter perspective, even within the narrow field of morphology.

Chomsky did not propose a theory of morphology; he merely suggested that there should be one, and that its properties, if he is correct in dividing morphology from syntax so sharply, should be very different from those of an adequate theory of syntax. I will attempt to elaborate such a theory. The theory which I will present bears, indeed, little resemblance to any prevalent theory of syntax. It will also encompass many phonological phenomena which cannot be easily incorporated into a reasonably narrow theory of phonology, and it will provide what I think is a unified account of morphological phenomena within a generative grammar. This unity is important. Critics of the new esthetic accuse its proponents of excessive rug-sweeping, clearing away so much data in the name of restricting the power of a grammar that the describable residue becomes miniscule. However, if we can show that what has been swept aside can be gathered up again, then we are vindicated in our vision.

2: Teleology

The purpose of this chapter is to explore further the general relationship between morphemes and words. In what sense do words consist of morphemes? Is there some constant relation between the two, as in syntax, where practically all sentences can be said to be synthetic entities, constructed out of words in a single way? We will see that words are very different from sentences, that their structures are much more varied, and that though there is a single principle governing the structure of most complex words, this principle must be applied in different ways to different classes of words. I will discuss these various classes.

Before going on to words, however, I must say a few things about morphemes, for though these units are basic to several aspects of the theory of language, their properties have been more asserted than studied, and since they are so central to our investigation we must be particularly careful that we know whereof we speak.

2.1. Trouble with Morphemes

The units into which words are analyzed, out of which they are composed, are termed *morphemes*. We will be concerned in this section with some problems concerning the defining characteristics of the morpheme, concentrating on a central premise of the approach which has been most pervasive in American linguistics. This premise is the definition of the morpheme as "the smallest individually meaningful element in the utterances of a language" (Hockett (1958, 123)). Accepting this premise entails that every polymorphemic word is a compositional entity. It is compositional in two senses, both semantically and structurally, the semantics being a function of the morphemes and the structure, just as a sentence is semantically compositional. Recent work has revived the truism that every word has its own idiosyncratic traits, some of which can be very erratic and elusive. (We are speaking here of derivational words; this waywardness does not extend to inflection.) If it is true of words that they are minimally meaningful, then what about the morpheme? Does it have no status at all, or can we define it other than semantically? The point of this section is to show that the latter question can be answered in the affirmative. Specifically, we will isolate a class of morphemes, show that there is no way in which the members of this class can be said to have any meaning at all, and then demonstrate that there are phonological criteria which allow us to isolate occurrences of these meaningless morphemes. The importance of this demonstration is two-fold. First, it shows us that any theory of "minimally meaningful element" is misguided. Second, it shows that despite this fact, it is still possible to construct a theory in which the morpheme plays a central role.

2.1.1. Minimal Signs

In order to understand what is at stake here, we must first have a better understanding of what is meant by *minimal meaningful element*. This entails a short review of de Saussure's concept of the *minimal sign*. The sign is one of the most basic concepts of linguistics, and the literature on the subject is vast. Nor is the definition of the sign a closed matter. I will adopt in this discussion what I think is an orthodox view, where orthodox does not, of course, mean totally uncontroversial.[1]

The minimal meaningful unit of a language is the basic, minimal, Saussurean sign (cf. de Saussure (1949)). The sign is an arbitrary union of the semantic and the phonetic. So the sign *dog* has a meaning and a sound; one cannot exist without the other; they are arbitrarily united. Arbitrarily, because there is nothing in the sound which dictates its meaning, and vice versa, except social convention. The sound may change and the meaning remain, or the meaning may change and the sound remain.

Out of the minimal signs we can construct composite signs. These signs are not arbitrary. Their meanings may be predicted from their structure and the minimal signs out of which they are constructed. Sentences are composite signs.

It is sometimes argued that there are different degrees of arbitrariness. A sign like *dog* is completely arbitrary. However, there are other signs whose sounds, we feel, have some intrinsic connections with their meanings. Onomatopoetic words, and those which involve phonetic symbolism (cf. Marchand (1969, 398 ff.)), like *slurp* and *quack*, are said to be partially *motivated* (nonarbitrary) because of this intrinsic connection. The class of partially motivated signs also includes composite items whose meanings can be partially, but not completely, derived from the meanings of their parts. Thus a sign which formally consists of the signs $a + b$, but whose meaning must be represented as $A + B + C$, that is, the meanings of a and b plus something else specific in addition, is sometimes said to be partially motivated. I will hold with de Saussure, and against Bally (1940) and Marchand (1969), that only fully motivated signs are to be counted as nonminimal, that partial motivation is not significant. Thus, any sign which is at all arbitrary is considered to be part of the basic inventory of signs.[2] Most of what follows is devoted to deciding what sorts of elements form this basic inventory.

2.1.2. Words

That there are minimal signs which are polymorphemic was first stressed as an important fact, at least within the framework of generative grammar, by Chomsky (1970). Chomsky noted that

---

[1] Readers may be interested in these controversies. Two good starting points are Spang-Hanssen (1954) and Koerner (1972).

[2] "Fully motivated" must not be confused with "fully meaningful". As Culicover (1972) has shown, some signs are inherently unspecified in such a way as to cause any utterance containing them to be highly, perhaps infinitely, ambiguous. The sentence *One more can of beer, and I'm leaving* (Culicover (1972)) is an instance of such an ambiguous entity. "What about that can of beer?" we ask. "Anything," is the reply. The point is that the meaning of the entire sentence is somehow partially unspecified. It is probable that all linguistic entities are not fully meaningful in this sense; all sentences are ambiguous, hence the poetic function. Instances such as these, however, differ fundamentally from those where two items a and b are concatenated and the concatenation does not mean '$a + b$ + infinite ambiguity' but rather '$a + b + c$', i.e. instances where some specific isolable constant part of the meaning of a concatenation cannot be derived from that of its parts. It is in these latter cases that motivation or arbitrariness is relevant.

much of derivational morphology is semantically irregular and should not be handled in the syntax. Out of this remark there developed two hypotheses. The *strong lexicalist hypothesis* of Jackendoff (1972) excludes all morphological phenomena from the syntax. This means that the syntax cannot relate *some* and *any*, or *ever* and *never*, and that inflection, if it is referred to in the syntax, must be handled by some sort of filter. The version of the *lexicalist hypothesis* which is more widely accepted than this one, but which to my knowledge has never been explicitly formulated in print, is that derivational morphology is never dealt with in the syntax, although inflection is, along with other such "morphological" matters as *Do* Support, Affix Hopping, Clitic Rules, i.e. all of "grammatical morphology". This seems to be the position of, for example, Chomsky (1973).[3] This latter hypothesis, which I will assume, does not say that derivational processes are always irregular and that their semantics is always noncompositional. Nor does it exclude from the domain of the syntax only irregular derivational phenomena as Chomsky (1970) says one might do. It says rather that derivational phenomena are always separate from the syntax, regardless of their regularity. Postal (1969) presents very convincing evidence for this hypothesis.[4] Translated into a Saussurean framework, the hypothesis says that for the purposes of syntax, the word (sans infection)[5] is the minimal sign.[6] This hypothesis says nothing about intraword phenomena and relations; they may or may not be regular. Of course the main reason for the adoption of the hypothesis in the first place was semantic irregularity, and we must develop a theory of derivational morphology which allows for, and hopefully even predicts and accounts for, this observed irregularity.

I will now present evidence that the word is a minimal sign, not merely for the purposes of the syntax. To do this, I will show that below the level of the word we encounter morphemes which, while they must be assumed to be real linguistic elements, have no meaning

---

[3] For example, it is stated that the factors into which a string may be analyzed by a transformation may include "morphological material". As far as I can tell, this means inflectional and other "grammatical" material.

[4] In the work cited, Postal also provides arguments against the lexicalist point of view. The latter arguments are not convincing to me. Similar arguments by Corum (1973) are discussed by Browne (1974).

[5] In general, throughout the rest of this work, *word* should be taken to mean 'word sans inflection' or *lexeme* in the sense of Matthews (1974).

[6] One might think that the idiom, a unit which has long mystified linguists, is an arbitrary sign which occurs at a higher syntactic level than that of the word. However, idioms differ from words in the following curious manner. An idiom is generally ambiguous between its literal (sometimes nonsensical) sense and its arbitrary "idiomatic" sense. If John kicked the bucket, he either kicked some previously specified bucket or he died. Complex words do not enjoy such a consistent ambiguity between constructible and arbitrary senses. Take the word *recital*. If we were to attempt to construct its meaning out of that of its parts, as we did for the literal interpretation of *John kicked the bucket*, we might arrive at something like 'the act(ion) of reciting' as an interpretation. But this word has, for me, no such interpretation. It has only an arbitrary sense, that of 'public performance, generally of music, generally by one person'.

The ambiguous nature of idioms makes them especially attractive material for punsters. The following examples from Milligan, Secombe, and Sellers (1956) are characteristic of the genre:

(i) Convict Eccles fell into a bucket of wet cement and looks like becoming a hardened criminal.

(ii) Q. How do you repel boarders?
A. Stop changing the bed linen.

Interplay between the literal and arbitrary sense of morphologically complex words, in contrast, is rarely found outside of Alexandrian poetry and the writings of Aldous Huxley.

which can be assigned independently of each of the individual words in which they occur. This demonstration is not a novelty. The most extended and formalized argument that I know of in favor of the point I am making is in Hervey and Mulder (1973).

2.1.3. Morphemes

2.1.3.1. Cranberry Morphs. There is in English a class of *hapax legomena*, morphemes which only occur in one English word. They are often called *cranberry morphs*. Consider the following list:

(1) cranberry   boysenberry   huckleberry

Since the words in our list are all names of berries, we may isolate this last unit as a meaningful morpheme. We are left with the items in (2):

(2) #cran#   #boysen#   #huckle#

None of these items occurs either independently or in any other words than those in (1). There is thus no noncircular way of assigning meanings to the morphemes in (2). Their meanings are intimately connected with those of the individual words in which they occur. As Hervey and Mulder note (1973, 45), "... a sign is only analyzable into two or more constituents in a grammar, if *each* of these constituents can be identified *as a sign*." Of course, one can ignore problems of circularity and assign a meaning to the item in question. It is then merely an accident that this fully meaningful item occurs only in one word. However, there are cases in which such a simple solution is not possible.

2.1.3.2. Other Berries. As noted above, it is possible to assign a meaning to items such as *#cran#*, simply because they do occur only in one word. With other names of berries, however, this simple device will not work. Consider the following list:

(3) strawberry   blueberry
     blackberry   gooseberry

By removing *berry* again, we can isolate the morphemes in (4):

(4) #straw#   #blue#
     #black#   #goose#

As opposed to the items in (2), these occur elsewhere than as parts of the names of berries; in fact, they occur as independent words. However, when they do appear as independent words, they have meanings which bear no relation to the meanings they might be assigned in (4). For example, one might think that a blackberry is black. However, not all black berries are blackberries, and furthermore, many blackberries are green or red (a fact also noted by Hervey and Mulder). There is therefore no way to assign a meaning to the item *black* which will be valid both when it occurs as an independent word and when it occurs in the word *blackberry*. The same holds for *blueberry*. The connection between geese and gooseberries or between straw and strawberries is not very apparent. The problem here is that we cannot resort to the simple ruse of assigning the items in (4) constant meanings, for they do occur elsewhere than in the words in (3), but with meanings which are totally incompatible with those we would like to assign to them on the basis of the meaning of the corresponding word in (3).

It is possible to get around this problem of a morpheme having different meanings in different words without entirely giving up the claim that morphemes are meaningful. The basic tack is to give morphemes underdetermined meanings, with contextually determed allo-meanings. This is essentially the solution which Chomsky (1970) adopts. In order to handle idiosyncratic semantic differences in verb-noun pairs like *refuse-refusal*, he says that "the lexical entry may specify that semantic features are in part dependent on the choice of one or another of these categorial features" (noun or verb) (1970, 190). To the extent that these dependencies are regular and syntactically motivated, there is virtue in such a device, or a similar redundancy convention, but to the extent that they are idiosyncratic, which many of them are, the device merely serves to obscure the truth, that it is the words which are idiosyncratic. Though this system may allow us to preserve the idea that morphemes are meaningful, it is only at the level of the individual word that these meanings can be fully specified.

In the particular case with which we are dealing, the device of underspecification and contextual filling leads to a particularly unsatisfying result. Since, as noted, some blackberries are red, and since something cannot be both black and red at the same time, the two allo-meanings of *#black#* will be contradictory and will share almost no semantic features (color?). Allowing a device which permits such a situation is very dangerous; it essentially gives homophony as the only criterion for deciding whether two things are instances of the same meaningful entity.[7]

One might also go entirely the opposite route. Thus one could claim that the various instances of *#black#* are completely unrelated, each a different morpheme. This rids us of the problem of morphemes with underspecified meanings, though we are still left with the circularity problem; is it the word or the morpheme which specifies the meaning? The next set of data bears on this theory.

2.1.3.3. Prefix=Stem (latinate). The last two sets of data consisted of what are traditionally called "partially motivated" forms. There was one element, *berry*, whose meaning was relatively constant, and another, which in a sense told us what sort of berry we were dealing with, but which never occurred, or never occurred with the same sense, outside of the particular word with which we were dealing. This next set of data differs from these in having no fixed element.

The data set consists of the latinate verbs with bound stems and prefixes which are always stressed on the stem. In the system of SPE this class is marked phonologically by the presence of a special boundary, =, between the prefix and the stem. Examples of such verbs are *refuse*, *convene*, and *inject*. I will not discuss verbs such as *suffer*, *proffer*, or *differ*, which diverge in their stress patterns from other prefixed verbs with bound stems, and for which no = boundary is posited. Nor will I discuss verbs such as *re#fuse* ('fuse again'), in which there is a # boundary

---

[7] There is a basic dissimilarity between this device and the one I alluded to in footnote (1). There underspecification resulted in infinite ambiguity (infiniguity?), which is not the case here.

in the system of SPE. For this class (x = y) it is possible to demonstrate that neither the prefix nor the stem has any fixed meaning.

First the stem. Consider the verbs in (5):

(5)
X=fer	*X=mit*	*X=sume*	*X=ceive*	*X=duce*
refer	remit	resume	receive	reduce
defer	demit		deceive	deduce
prefer		presume		
infer				induce
confer	commit	consume	conceive	conduce
transfer	transmit			transduce
	submit	subsume		
	admit	assume		adduce
	permit		perceive	

Let us presume for the moment that the prefixes in (5) have constant meanings, much as the *berry* of (1) and (3). Is it possible to extract any common meanings, however minimal, from the different occurrences of each stem? At first glance, if we merely compare pairs of verbs, one might be tempted to think so. *Confer* and *transfer* might appear to share something, similarly *remit* and *submit*, *conceive* and *perceive*, *assume* and *presume*, *induce* and *deduce*. However, if we attempt to extend our hypotheses beyond these select pairs by extracting the common sense from each and assigning it to the other verbs in the particular stem, the result is nonsense. What even vague sense does *prefer* share with *confer* and *transfer*? or *commit* with *remit* and *submit*? or *receive* with *conceive* and *perceive*? or *consume* with *presume* and *assume*? or *reduce* with *induce* and *deduce*? None. There is no meaning which can be assigned to any of these stems and combined with the presumably constant meanings of the prefixes in a consistent way to produce the meanings of all the verbs in that stem. Each stem occurs in different verbs, but never with the same sense. Rather, the sense is determined by the individual verb.

As suggested above, one might attempt to reduce the whole problem to cranberries (with, of course, the accompanying problems of that class) by calling each occurrence of a given stem a different morpheme. This system denies any linguistic reality to the stems and replaces each of them by a list of homophones, each having its own meaning and each occurring with only one, perhaps even two, prefixes. In such a system one would not have, for instance, a stem *mit* which occurred in all the relevant words in (9); rather, one would have many homophonous stems, $mit_1, mit_2, \ldots mit_n$. This system would be fine if these stems had nothing at all in common. The problem is that all occurrences of the stem *mit* do share a common feature which is not predictable from any general phonological properties of the sequence [mit]. As will be carefully documented in chapter 5, all instances of the latinate stem *mit* exhibit the same phonologically arbitrary variant (allomorph) before the suffixes +*ion*, +*ory*, +*or*, +*ive*, +*able*. The details of the relevant argument are given in chapter 5. For the moment we can look at the following paradigm:

(6) permit   permission   permissive
     remit   remission   remissory
     excrete   excretion   excretive
     assert   assertion   assertive
     digest   digestion   digestive
     prohibit   prohibition   prohibitive

The last column reveals the difference between verbs of the form $X=mit$ and other verbs with final t before the suffixes in question. *Mit* always takes the form *mis* here, and the change of t to s in this environment is confined to this one stem. There are no exceptions to this rule either way.

This regularity, or the factors which condition it, cannot be phonological, but must be stated on another linguistic level, the level of the stem or morpheme. Proof of this assertion is the fact that other instances of the phonological sequence [mit], which are not instances of the latinate stem *mit*, do not show up as [mis] in the relevant environment. So we find *vomit/vomitory*. In the word *vomit*, there is no reason to presume that we are dealing with a prefix *vo* and a stem *mit*; in fact, there is good reason to believe that we are not: *vo* never shows up as a prefix elsewhere, and the stress pattern gives us no evidence of a boundary, or at least of the sort of boundary for which there could be evidence. The alternation in question is therefore restricted to the latinate stem *mit*. This means that all the items which in the theory in question were mere homophones, $mit_1, \ldots mit_n$, must be at some level instances of the same thing. Otherwise there is no way to express the fact that all occurrences of *mit* exhibit the same allomorphy. There is good evidence that the level at which the rule embodying the facts in question must be stated is that of the morpheme. First of all it can be shown that a feature such as [+*latinate*], which governs among other things what sorts of affixes can be attached to a word, is a property of morphemes. Second, the sort of rule that changes t to s in the relevant environment here is a rule which applies to a morpheme and not to any other linguistic level, lower or higher. *Mit* is therefore a morpheme, though it has no meaning. Nor is *mit* the only case. As we shall see in chapter 5, there are many stems which undergo rules of allomorphy.

It appears, then, that there is something fundamentally wrong with the theory of many homophonous *mits*, for there is good evidence that we are indeed dealing with one morpheme. This turns us back to the allo-meaning theory, with its problems of underspecified meanings and circularity, or to the theory that morphemes are not minimal signs. The allo-meaning theory had some plausibility with reference to the preceding sets of data (*cranberry, blackberry*, etc.), mainly because, as noted, we always had one constant element with a relatively perspicuous meaning, and we could as a result attribute the residue of the meaning of each word to the problematic morpheme. However, when we look at the prefixes, we find that (just as with the stems) there is no constant meaning which can be attributed to any of them. How, then, are we to segment the meaning of the individual words in a principled manner?

Consider the following list:

(7)   *re=X*   *con=X*   *in=X*   *de=X*
      repel   compel   impel
      remit   commit   demit
      refer   confer   infer   defer
      resume   consume
      receive   conceive   deceive
      reduce   conduce   induce   deduce

Though it is more likely that one could attribute more commonality of meaning to occurrences of some of these prefixes than one could to any of the stems, there is no general meaning which can be assigned to any of them. Thus one might try to assign to *re* a meaning 'back', and a large number of the verbs of the form *re=X* have something to do with 'back' (cf. Williams (1973)). What about *receive*, though? Or consider *reduce* in the following sentence:

(8) The government reduced the size of the quart from 32 to 31 ounces, in an effort to stop inflation.

Since the quart never was less than 32 ounces, there is no way in which 'back' can be involved in the meaning of *reduce* here.

Now, since we know from (7) that *re=* has no fixed meaning, and we know from (5) that *duce* has no fixed meaning, how are we to segment the meaning of *reduce* into two parts, one associated with *re=* and the other with *duce*, in a principled manner? We can't. The word *principled* is important here. A priori, any word can be split in two and each part given a meaning. I can divide *apple* into *a* and *pl*, and give each of them part of the meaning of the whole word. However, we prefer to reject this solution, for by allowing such an analysis we would reduce the predictive power of a theory to zero, as noted above. It is unfalsifiable. Thus the fact that the allo-meaning theory must be made so strong in these cases that its empirical validity is reduced to zero forces us to fall back on the only position left to us: there are morphemes which have no meaning. The hypothesis that morphemes are the "minimal meaningful elements of language" cannot be maintained even in any of its most contorted variants. In many cases this role of the minimal sign must be moved one level up, to the level of the word. The sign gravitates to the word.

Note that we have not abandoned the concept of the morpheme. It still remains, but not always as a sign.

2.1.3.4. *A Similar Class.* The same argument as was made in 2.1.3.3 can be made for the following set of data, which comprises a much smaller though more striking set of prefixed verbs:

(9)   understand/stood   undertake/took
      withstand/stood
                              partake/took

There is no way to relate the putative meanings of *stand* in its two occurrences, nor those of *take*. Nor can the meaning of *stand*, in *understand* at least, be related to any of the multifarious meanings of the free verb *stand*. Similarly for the prefixes *under*, *with*, and *par*. However, in the case of the stems, we must be able to encode the fact that they always show the same variant in the past tense form. Nor is there any way in which this variant can be viewed as phonologically conditioned. It must be conditioned by some abstract property which is common to all occurrences of the meaningless entity *stand* or *take*.

2.1.3.5. Defining the Morpheme. The morpheme is traditionally defined as the minimal sign: an arbitrary constant union of sound and meaning. This definition must be adjusted to include such morphemes as *mit*, which have no constant meaning. Now, *mit* is clearly a constant phonetic string (at the level of the input to the phonology). It is also arbitrarily linked to something. However, it is linked not to a meaning but to a phonological rule, the rule which changes *t* to *s* before *+ion*, *+ive*, *+ory*, and *+or*, only in the morpheme *mit* (cf. *vomitory*, **vomissory*). The original definition of the morpheme has three aspects: constant form, arbitrary link, constant meaning. In order to include *mit* in the class of morphemes, we need only broaden the third, that of constant meaning, to include a phonological operation as well. This broadened definition will allow us to include *stand* and *take* also.[8] The rule to which they are arbitrarily linked spells out the past tense.[9]

That I include a meaning and a phonological rule in the same class of entities, and speak of mere broadening in doing so, may strike some as odd. But I only wish to point, perhaps a little dramatically, to what is essential about a morpheme: not that it mean, but rather merely that we be able to recognize it. A morpheme is a phonetic string which can be connected to a linguistic entity outside that string. What is important is not its meaning, but its arbitrariness. This is close to the position of Harris (1951).

2.1.4. Trouble with Words?

2.1.4.1. Cranberry Words. There are words which, like cranberry morphs, concatenate only with specific words and not with syntactic classes. For example, the noun *headway* occurs only as the direct object of the verb *make*, just as *cran* occurs only in *cranberry*. However, there is a difference in the manner of concatenation. On the phonological and syntactic surface, *cran* can only appear in one specific place, directly before *berry*. However, *headway* does not necessarily appear directly after *make* on the surface. Rather, it is the head of its underlying object NP, and as such it may be modified and even moved about:

(10) We haven't made much headway lately.

(11) Are we making any sort of headway here?

(12) There isn't much headway being made.

(13) The only headway we were making was illusory.[10]

---

[8] Not all instances of the phonological string *stand* are instances of the morpheme *stand*. This can be seen from such examples as *grandstanded*.

[9] According to Harris (1951) the ablaut rule itself is a morpheme, an allomorph of the past tense morpheme usually spelled out as *ed*.

[10] Within an orthodox analysis of relative clauses *headway* is never, strictly speaking, the object of *make* in this sentence (cf. Vergnaud (1974)).

Because it occurs in these different environments, we can isolate other properties of *headway* than the fact that it is an arbitrary phonological string. It is a noun. It is not a count noun (**headways*). It is not animate (*...headway...it*). Thus we can say things about *headway* which are not dependent on *make*, and which have something to do with its meaning. This is not true of *cran*, and it is the complete interdependence of *cran* and *berry* which forces us to conclude that in the strictest sense the former cannot be meaningful.[11] The point is that because *cran* is completely isolated from the syntax by its occurrence inside only the one word, there is no way in which it can have syntactic (and hence semantic) properties of its own. Because it is a noun and the head of a syntactic phrase, *headway* is not so insulated. As the head of a phrase it must, perforce, have syntactic properties, some of which may be related to meaning properties.

2.1.4.2. The Numerous Verbs Stand. I have argued that the various instances of *stand* in (9) could not be related to one another semantically, though they must be regarded as instances of the same entity because of their shared irregularity (*stand/stood*). It seems possible to argue exactly the same point from the various occurrences of *stand* as an independent verb. Many of the uses of the verb *stand* cannot be related semantically, and yet the same irregular past form always appears. Consider the following sentences:

(14)   We stood there for a while.

(15)   We stood the chairs in a corner.

(16)   I stood it as long as I could, and then left.

Though one might conceivably attempt to relate the verbs of (14) and (15) in some manner, perhaps even systematically, I cannot see how either of these two could be related to the verb in (16). However, though the meaning of this verb cannot be systematically related to the others, its form is. Therefore, extending the argument of 2.1.3.4 to this class, one might wish to say that the word *stand* is a unit, but it has no meaning. There is no difference between morphemes and words.

With regard to meaning, the same sorts of arguments hold here as we observed in 2.1.4.1. The various verbs in the above sentences have different subcategorizations, and from subcategorization we can go to meaning. Therefore the individual verbs are not meaningless or indeterminable as to their meaning. They each comprise a separate entry in the lexicon.

The problem is accounting for a property which they share and which has nothing to do with their meanings. This is the common irregularity of their past tense forms. It is here that our expanded definition of the morpheme comes into play. By this new definition, all occurrences of the string *stand* which alternate systematically with *stood* in the past tense are instances of the same *morpheme*. This means that the various verbs *stand* of (14)–(16) are all instances of a single morpheme, the same morpheme which occurs in *understand* and *withstand*. However, they are not instances of the same sign, for, as we have seen, a morpheme need not be a sign at all.

[11] The problem of idioms intersects with this one.

This distinction allows us to represent both the sameness and the difference of the items in question. The notions *morpheme* and *sign*, as defined, are not really notions of the same sort. Two words can be instances of the same morpheme. In addition, freeing the morpheme from the requirement that it be meaningful, which we have found to be necessary, allows us to use it to account for phenomena which, in other theories, could not be related (no prevalent theory which I am aware of is capable of encoding formal similarities of this arbitrary sort among words unless they are accompanied by semantic similarities). The numerous verbs *stand* thus present no problem for our revised view of the morpheme; rather, they can be much more satisfactorily accommodated than they had been previously.

2.1.5. A Historical Note on Inflection

It should not be terribly surprising that morphemes are not the "minimal meaningful elements" they have been purported to be. This conception of a morpheme is very intimately tied in with certain structuralist assumptions. It is, in part at least, a consequence of a simple view of the relationship between sound and meaning and the mappings which express this relation.

When dealing with inflection, this type of system is especially difficult to justify. Even very early, attempts by Hockett (1947) and Bloch (1947) to apply to real data the definition of a morpheme as a one-to-one mapping between meaning and sound led to very bizarre and counterintuitive results (cf. Nida (1948) for criticism of the two works cited above). Harris (1948) discusses the problems that a paradigmatic set of data presents for a theory in which the morpheme is the basic meaningful element. Chomsky (1965) made essentially the same point as Harris twenty years later, when he introduced the complex symbol and syntactic feature as a way of treating paradigmatic and crossclassified phenomena. In a system like Chomsky's, the traditional concept of a morpheme as a one-to-one mapping between form and meaning is nullified. Chomsky makes this point explicitly and argues for the virtue of his system over the old one with regard to the treatment of inflection (1965, 170-174).

Thus, rejecting the morpheme as a basis for a theory of derivational morphology, at least in its definition as a minimally meaningful unit, is not the radical step one might think it to be. As a basis for accounting for inflectional phenomena, it has long been under attack. We must now develop a theory of morphology which does not crucially depend on the morpheme as a basic meaning-bearing element.

2.2. Word Formation

The goal of this section is to sketch out the underpinnings of a theory of morphology. In view of the preceding section, we will assume that such a theory must not include the premise that morphemes are necessarily meaningful.

2.2.1. Possible and Actual Words

Just as the simplest goal of a syntax is the enumeration of the class of possible sentences of a language, so the simplest task of a morphology, the least we demand of it, is the enumeration of the class of possible words of a language. The greatest difference between the syntax and morphology with respect to this enumeration is that in derivational morphology there is a distinction to be made between the classes of possible words and actual words.[12]

This difference has long been recognized. Early critics of generative grammar (Zimmer (1964), Schachter (1962)) pointed out that there are many words which a grammar can generate in a language which, accidentally and unsystematically, never appear. This very pervasive phenomenon, they point out, cannot be handled in a morpheme-based grammar which does not posit an independent level of words, distinct from higher syntactic entities, as prelexicalist grammars indeed did not. Of the few substantial works on morphology within generative grammar, two have contained proposals, essentially the same in their content, designed to deal with exactly this distinction between possible and actual. Botha (1968) and Halle (1973a) have suggested that, in addition to the list of morphemes of a language and the rules of morphology, which concatenate these morphemes into possible words, there must exist a list of actual words, a dictionary, which they see as a sort of filter on the output of the morphology. Within a morpheme-based theory of morphology such as theirs, there are then two lexicons: a list of morphemes and their meanings which, together with the morphology, defines the class of possible words of a language; and a word lexicon. The actual words are a subset of the possible.

But words are peculiar, not only in that not all of those that should exist actually do, but also in that those which do exist do not always mean what they are supposed to mean, or even look like what they are supposed to look like. Words, once formed, persist and change; they take on idiosyncrasies, with the result that they are soon no longer generable by a simple algorithm of any generality. The word gravitates toward the sign. The actual words of a language, the members of the set of dictionary entries, are as a result not a subset of the items which are generated by a regular morphology, one which generates words and their meanings out of meaningful morphemes.

This is the basic trouble with morphemes. Because words, though they may be formed by regular rules, persist and change once they are in the lexicon, the morphemes out of which words seem to have been formed, and into which they seem to be analyzable, do not have constant meanings and in some cases have no meaning at all. It is this persistence which forces us to adopt a lexicalist hypothesis.

Halle noticed this problem and suggested that the dictionary should contain not only the actual words, but also that the idiosyncrasies of each word, if there are any, be listed there as well. These idiosyncrasies would include the phonological and syntactic exception features which a word might have, as well as its semantic and syntactic peculiarities, i.e. those semantic and syntactic properties not provided by the general rules of the morphology. A problem which immediately arises, even in this less rigid framework, in which it is at least tacitly admitted that arbitrary meanings can be assigned at the word level, is that there are words

[12] In the realm of phonotactics there exist words which are, in a certain sense, impossible. Thus, though the initial cluster *sf* is systematically banned from English words, in the sense that it could not be accepted in newly coined nonsense words, it does occur in a fair number of Greek borrowings: *sphere, sphinx, sphincter*, etc. We do not want to say that *sf* is a possible initial cluster in English, yet it exists in actual words. Similar facts are true, to a lesser extent, in morphology.

which are so idiosyncratic that their meanings are totally divorced from what is expected by the general rule. In Halle's system, a word can mean more than it is expected to mean, but it is difficult to see how it could mean something completely different from what its predicted meaning is without severely damaging the rules of the system or weakening it to the point that its predictive powers are obliterated. For example, the word *transmission*, which according to the general rules of the morphology should be an abstract nominal meaning something like 'the action of transmitting', means nothing of the sort when it refers to a car's transmission. It does not just mean more than it is supposed to. In a system such as Halle's, in which a word is provided with a meaning by general rules and this meaning can be expanded upon, words like this are very problematic.

The important thing we do learn from Halle's work is that there will always be a large number of words in a language which, because of their irregularities, must be entered in a lexicon. Since we are attempting to enumerate the class of possible words of a language, this lexicon already takes care of a large part of our task.

However, the list of words which a speaker has at his command at a given moment is not closed. The speaker always has the capacity to make up new words, which he can then add to his repertoire. It thus remains the task of a morphology to tell us what sort of new words a speaker can form. Note that we have suggested that the gross irregularities which words in the dictionary often exhibit are due to their persistence, to the mere fact that they are listed. It seems reasonable to assume that such gross irregularities are not characteristic of the new words which a speaker makes up; simply because they have not existed long, these words have not had any opportunity to become fixed in some idiosyncrasy. We will assume, then, that there are regular and interesting rules for making up new words, and we will turn now to the task of describing these rules.

Of course, we do not ask of a good theory of morphology merely that it perform this one task. Though they are idiosyncratic, the words in the dictionary do exhibit regularities; they do have structure. Morphemes, even though they may not be what they have been purported to be, are recognizable. Nor does a speaker make up all the new words he encounters. He hears words he has never heard before, recognizes them as words of his language, if they are, and has intuitions about their meaning and structure. A good theory of morphology should tell us something about these matters as well, and to the extent that they seem to be related to one another and to the mechanism for making up new words, the theory we present should express this relationship.

2.2.2. Types of New Words

We must determine what sorts of new words can be coined. The restriction here is very clear and pervasive. The only classes of words to which new words can be added by coining are the major lexical categories: noun (N), adjective (Adj), verb (V), adverb (Adv). New coinings may not be added to the various "grammatical" categories: pronoun, determiner, quantifier, conjunction, preposition, particle, modal, auxiliary, etc. This fact can be related to the distinction between inflectional and derivational morphology, but I will not try to go into details of that relationship here.[13]

Nice confirmation of the restriction of new coinings to major lexical categories is provided by the opening lines of Lewis Carroll's "Jabberwocky", which are repeated below (the italics are mine):

'Twas *brillig*, and the *slithy toves*
Did *gyre* and *gimble* in the *wabe*:
All *mimsy* were the *borogoves*,
And the *mome raths outgrabe*.

All the words which are members of major lexical categories have been italicized. All other words are "grammatical". If we accept Humpty Dumpty's analysis, then all of the italicized words, and none of the others, are new coinages. This accords perfectly with the claim being made here.

2.2.3. What are New Words Coined From?

2.2.3.1. Oddities. The italicized words in the verse of "Jabberwocky" above are all rather unusual coinages. Those whose basis is not completely opaque are *blendings* (cf. Marchand (1969, 451–454)) or, as Carroll calls them, *portmanteau words*, formed by merging parts of words into a word which meets the phonotactic restrictions of the language. More transparent examples are *smog*, from *smoke* and *fog*, and *chunnel*, from *channel* and *tunnel*.

A related type of coining is that of *letter words* and *syllable words*, collectively known as *acronyms*. Examples are *NATO*, *radar*, and *futhorc*. This type is almost unknown in the languages of the world and was uncommon in our own before this century. It is even possible that the modern use of it can be traced back to that of the Hebrew scholarly tradition, where the names of sages were abbreviated by means of such a device (*rashi* = *ra*bbi *sh*lomo *ben yich*aq; *rambam* = *ra*bbi *m*oshe *b*en *m*aimon). It does, in any case, presuppose an alphabet. At present it is most common in the official languages of the major imperialist powers. The device is, in short, very unusual and certainly not a universal fact of language.

These two devices form words which have no recognizable internal structure or constituents. This makes them opaque, and hence uncommon. The logic of the *hence* is that when we hear a word whose meaning we do not have any clues to, unless this word denotes an important

---

[13] Note that the latter, grammatical, categories, are not closed. They may acquire new members, but by a sort of drift. So it has often been noted that a word like *near* is an adjective on its way to becoming a preposition. In other languages, prepositions can sometimes be traced back to nominal forms. Nor does drift affect only nonlexical categories. The noun *fun* is on its way to becoming an adjective:

(i) That's no/not fun.

The reverse course is being traversed by *good*:

(ii) That's not/no good.

A complete theory of language must account for this sort of thing; however, because it is a phenomenon involving existing words and the changes they go through, I think we can safely exclude it from the domain of morphology as here defined (though see Ullmann (1962) for observations on lexical drift).

thing, we will have difficulty retaining it.[14]

2.2.3.2. Words from Morphemes. Another type of device which is also uncommon consists of the stringing together of morphemes with, of course, appropriate restrictions on what morphemes go where: suffixes at the end, prefixes at the beginning, etc. This type of coining accords with the sort of morphology we are accustomed to believing in.

An example of such a coining is the word *transmote* (brought to my attention by Bob Fiengo), which has the structure [trans=mote]$_V$ and consists of the morphemes *trans* as in *transmit* and *mote* as in *emote*, in the latinate prefix stem pattern discussed in 2.1. The etymology of the word is curious. Officials of the Johnson administration needed a verb which would mean 'transfer from one position to another', but would have neither negative nor laudatory connotations. *Transfer* is slightly negative, and *demote* and *promote* both imply a change in rank; hence *transmote*, with the *trans* of *transfer* and the *mote* of the other two.

What is important to note about *transmote* is that despite its seeming structure its meaning is not completely clear until explicated. Only when it is compared with *transfer*, *demote*, and *promote* is it possible even to begin to make an intelligent guess at its sense. The word thus resembles a blending like *chunnel* (*channel tunnel*), which is derived from other words, but not at all transparently. The lack of semantic transparency should not be surprising to anyone who has read the section on meaning and morphemes in 2.1. There I took pains to show that exactly these classes of prefixes and stems have no meaning. They are not signs. Since the parts have no independent meaning, the meaning of the whole is unclear. It follows from this, by the short argument given above, that the sort of word formation of which *transmote* is a product will be as sporadic as blending. In fact, I think we can reasonably claim that the two devices are really one: take two words, stick them together, and chop out the middle.

2.2.3.3. Word-based Morphology. I have dealt rather hastily with several types of word-formation processes which I claim are really one. The main characteristic of this type of word formation is the fact that the meaning of a word formed by such a process can never be derived regularly. By a simplistic argument, I have also connected this characteristic with lack of productivity. I will not discuss these opaque processes any further.

It remains to establish what sorts of word-formation processes can be productive. This brings us to the main thesis of this work (and many previous ones):

> *Hypothesis*
> All regular word-formation processes are word-based. A new word is formed
> by applying a regular rule to a single already existing word. Both the new
> word and the existing one are members of major lexical categories.

Any theory of which this hypothesis is a basic tenet we will call a theory of *word-based morphology*. In the rest of this work, I will try to develop a relatively detailed version of such a theory.

---

[14] Words which denote important things tend to be monomorphemic.

2.2.3.4. Word Formation Rules. The regular rules referred to above will be termed *Word Formation Rules* (*WFR*). Such a rule specifies a set of words on which it can operate. This set, or any member of this set, we will term the *base* of that rule. Every WFR specifies a unique phonological operation which is performed on the base.[15] Every WFR also specifies a syntactic label and subcategorization for the resulting word, as well as a semantic reading for it, which is a function of the reading of the base. Chapter 4 will be devoted to a more detailed discussion of the general form and characteristics of WFRs.

It is a fact that almost all new words are produced by WFRs. I will give only one example: from the adjective *communal* I form the verb *communalize*, by the WFR of #*ize* attachment. I know what this word means, since I know what its base means, and the rule is regular. *X#ize* can be paraphrased roughly as 'make X'. It is quite a different case from *transmote*. From *communalize*, in turn, I form the abstract action nominal *communalization*, by the WFR of +*Ation* attachment. This word too is transparent in its meaning.

Note that WFRs do not operate on anything less than a word, i.e. on morphemes. As demonstrated, not all morphemes are meaningful. Since regular rules can only derive meaningful words from meaningful bases, it follows of course that meaningless morphemes cannot serve as bases for any such rules. But I have not specified meaningfulness as a criterion for serving as the base of a WFR. If there are meaningful morphemes, and I have not argued that such entities never exist, the theory as formulated does not permit them to serve as the base of any WFR. This is of course an empirical claim. In 2.2.5 I will discuss a class of words which do not seem to be derived from existing ones. Such a class would be counterevidence to the claim being made here, if indeed one could show that these words were so derived. In this particular case, there is good evidence that the base of the rules is a class of existing words.

One important peculiarity of the conception of the rules of word formation I am outlining here is that I do not view these rules as applying every time the speaker of a language speaks. They are rules for making up new words which may be added to the speaker's lexicon. We can think of them as once-only rules. They are thus very different from the rules of the syntax and the phonology which must apply in the derivation of every sentence. This has been pointed out by other people in other contexts (e.g. Halle (1973a)); however, it has normally been stated as an observation and not as a basic tenet of a theory of morphology.

2.2.3.5. Assumptions about the Lexicon. The rules of word formation are rules for generating words which may be stored in the dictionary of a language. The rules are a part of the grammar of that language. I assume that these rules are completely separate from the syntactic and phonological rules of the grammar. Thus when a WFR specifies a phonological operation, this operation is not merely indicated by the WFR in the form of some rule feature and then performed as a rule of the phonology. Rather, the phonological operation is part of the WFR itself.[16] The same position with regard to syntactic and semantic phenomena is a basic tenet of

---

[15] This operation usually consists of the addition of some affix. It can, however, be null, and it may be more subtle. The matter is discussed at some length in chapter 4.

[16] It may be that this claim has to be weakened in certain cases, specifically in the case of reduplication rules (cf. the discussion of reduplication rules in Tagalog in Carrier (1975)).

the extended standard theory of syntax, one of the central claims of which is that lexical insertion, at the level of the major lexical category, precedes all syntactic rules (cf. Postal (1969)).

A consequence of these assumptions is that each word may be entered in the dictionary as a fully specified separate item. It is possible, and not unusual, to conceive of a system in which all redundancies are removed from the entries and then somehow filled back in by general rule. Such an approach was long accepted in phonology, but because of certain difficulties associated with the particular notation being used (allowing features to be specified + or −, or given no specification) brought to light by Stanley (1967), this manner of dealing with redundancies was replaced by a system in which all phonological features were completely specified in the lexical entry for each word (or morpheme). Such a system is accepted and even presupposed by most leading contemporary phonologists (SPE, chapter 9; Kiparsky (1973)). There is good reason for not factoring out syntactic and semantic redundancies either. This will be discussed later, in the context of a method for dealing with morphological regularities in the dictionary.

I will assume, then, that each word in the dictionary is an independent item, fully specified. Dictionary entries are not dependent on one another, or on rules. Each one is a complete sign in itself.

2.2.4. Evidence for the Proposal

The theory proposed here is essentially based on an observation: new words are by and large formed from old ones by recognizable rules. This theory also has the advantage of ridding us of the central problem of a morpheme-based theory of morphology (though at present it does so at some expense, by removing from consideration all matters pertaining to words already in the dictionary).[17]

However, a good theory does more than avoid problems. It also helps us to understand and account for things which hitherto were inexplicable. I would now like to discuss two matters which the theory so far outlined helps us to understand: the phonological cycle and irregular back-formations.

2.2.4.1. The Phonological Cycle. The phonological cycle is a much talked about subject. Some suspect the validity of the entire concept, and many have criticized what they have felt to be unmotivated uses of the device. Cyclic phonological rules are dependent for their operation on labeled bracketings. They apply first to maximal strings which contain no labeled brackets, after which innermost brackets are erased (or equally, disregarded); then they apply to the next maximal string which contains no brackets; and so on (cf. SPE, chapter 2). The most principled objections to the cycle have been directed against the arbitrary and high-handed manner in which these labeled bracketings are sometimes determined.

---

[17] The theory is not specifically designed to avoid the problem of meaningless morphemes. As stressed above, words are formed from words, not "meaningful elements".

In an important article, Brame (1974) has attempted to answer these objections by proposing a general constraint on such bracketing. The basis for Brame's constraint is the observation that the string constituting the domain of every application of the cycle of rules "shows up elsewhere as an independent phonetic word sequence" (1974, 55).[18]

Brame's constraint is a formulation of his observation. Before stating the constraint, we need a definition (from Brame (1974, 56)):

Definition

Two strings in phonological representations are said to be *equipotent* if they are identical and at least one of the two is not represented as a proper substring in phonetic representations.

Brame proposes a *Natural Bracketing Hypothesis* (1974, 56):

For a substring ψ to be bracketed, it must be equipotent to a string σ.

Translated into simpler terms, and clearing up some ambiguities in the definition of equipotency (a proper substring of what? probably of a string bounded by ##...##), Brame's hypothesis says that only a string whose surface reflex shows up elsewhere as an independent word can be bracketed. There is a slight problem with this hypothesis. One wants to avoid bracketings like the following: [[fil]ter]. Yet such a bracketing meets the conditions which the hypothesis imposes: *fil* occurs elsewhere as an independent word. In order to avoid the possibility of this bracketing, Brame suggests that we adopt instead the following strong version of the above hypothesis (1974, 58):

Strong Natural Bracketing Hypothesis

For a substring ψ of a string ϕ to be bracketed, ψ must be equipotent to a string σ, and the meaning of ϕ must be a compositional function of the meaning of σ and $\phi - \psi$ (ϕ minus ψ).

This rules out the bracketing [[fil]ter].

The latter hypothesis, Brame notes, may be too strong,[19] but it is interesting.

---

[18] The phrase is ambiguous. An underlying phonological string of the form $x + y$ can be said to have a surface representation of the form XY, which will not always be identical to $x + y$. We will take the sense of Brame's observation to be that we may cycle on underlying x only if surface X is an independently occurring word. Another possible sense is that we may cycle on X just in case there is an independently occurring surface word of the form x, rather than of the form X, i.e. identical to the underlying rather than the surface form. It is difficult to tell which sense Brame intended.

[19] Brame lists some problematic forms from Maltese which, though they must be derived cyclically in his system, at least intuitively do not meet the strong hypothesis. u is the plural subject in the following forms:

nišorbu 'we drink'
titúlfu 'you pl. drink'

In Brame's system they must be derived from the following:

[[ni+šrob]+u]
[[ti+tlif]+u]

There is a cycle on u.

The question now naturally arises whether a constraint like that imposed by the Strong Hypothesis is a basic theoretical entity, or whether it falls out from more general principles. There obviously is some device which assigns these natural bracketings, and this device should have some other motivation than the mere fact that it assigns natural bracketings. Brame does not speculate on the nature of this device.

Within the theory of SPE, the input to the phonology is supplied by the syntax. The bracketing which defines the phonological cycle is basically that of the syntactic surface structure (with a few readjustments). Within that theory, therefore, there is independent justification for the bracketings in question. Within the lexicalist theory, however, the syntax does not extend below the level of the word and as a result cannot be called upon to generate any intraword bracketings. Since, in the earlier theory, the bracketing could be syntactically motivated, we expect that in the new theory whatever replaces the syntax at the level in question should assign the bracketing in question. This is of course the morphology.

Within the theory of morphology outlined above, a new word is always formed by performing some phonological operation on an already existing one. In most cases, the effect of this phonological operation will be the addition of some affix to the already existing word. This means, in effect, that the new word will contain the old. The meaning of the new word will also be a compositional function of the meaning of the word it contains. Since members of major lexical categories are always labeled (N, V, Adj, Adv), since all regular WFRs operate on such labeled words, and since there is no reason to assume that these labels are erased in the course of the application of a WFR, WFRs will, unless otherwise constrained, produce labeled bracketings in their output. It is clear that all the constraints imposed on intraword bracketings by the Natural Bracketing Hypothesis are direct consequences of this theory. In fact, given this theory, no other bracketing is possible. This is evidence of the highest order in favor of the central claims of the theory proposed.

Note that there is no reason to suppose that the sort of sporadic word formation discussed in 2.2.3.1 and 2.2.3.2 results in any kind of labeled bracketings. Thus a new word like *transmote* will not have a cyclic structure. Nor will such a word be bracketable according to Brame's hypothesis. As far as I know, words formed by such processes need never be treated in a cyclic fashion. This provides yet more evidence in favor of our theory, and in favor of the separation of word-formation devices into the two types.

Not all words have cyclic structure. There are sometimes even minimal pairs, the only difference between the members of which is the fact that one may be derived cyclically, the other not. Consider the following case, discussed by Brame. There are two words, *Prohibition* [proəbišən] and *prohibition* [prohibišən]: the first refers to a certain law or period in American history; the second is a deverbal action nominal. They are distinguished on the phonological surface by the fact that one has *h* followed by *i* where the other has *ə*. This difference can be accounted for if we give the two words the following underlying phonological forms:

spelling	surface	underlying
Prohibition	[proəbišən]	[pro=hibit+ion]$_N$
prohibition	[prohibišən]	[[pro=hibit+]$_V$+ion]$_N$

Thus the only difference between the two words is that one, and not the other, has cyclic structure. The superficial differences then fall out by regular rule. In the first word, a rule operates which elides *h* before an unstressed vowel, in this case *i*. Since it never receives stress, this *i* is later reduced to *ə* by the general rule of vowel reduction which operates on all unstressed lax vowels. In the second word, this same *i*, the one which follows *h*, will be stressed on the first cycle by the Primary Stress Rule as it would be in the verb (*prohibit*). Though the next vowel is stressed on the next cycle, and consequently receives the main stress by the Detail Rule (cf. Halle (1973c)),[20] there is still sufficient stress on the *i* following the *h* to prevent the application of the *h* elision rule (which only operates before an unstressed vowel), and also to prevent the *i* from being reduced. We see then that once the cyclic structure is imposed, all differences can be derived in a principled manner without recourse to exception features or special rules. There is in fact no other principled way to derive these two forms, and they provide powerful evidence for a theory which includes the notion of the cycle.

According to our theory of morphology, every new word, if it is derived by a regular rule, must have cyclic structure: that is, it must be bracketed internally. However, [proəbišən] has been shown not to have cyclic structure. This seems to be a problem for our theory. According to it, shouldn't all complex words be derived cyclically?

Remember that the rationale for discussing only literal word formation, i.e. coining, and not discussing the structure of words which were already in the dictionary, was the fact that the latter tend to be irregular, that is, to lose some of their appointed meaning and gain individual nuances. Such divergences from compositionality clearly do not take place in a linguistic vacuum, and it seems reasonable to suppose that they have structural correlates. Consider the two words under discussion. Clearly the first one, [proəbišən], is further in meaning from the verb *prohibit*. In fact, we would be hard pressed to find any systematic link between the two. The second noun, [prohibišən], is the derived action nominal of the verb, and its meaning is a compositional function of that of the verb. We have seen that this semantic difference is accompanied by a structural difference, in that [prohibišən] but not [proəbišən] has cyclic structure. In fact, in general, when we find two words which differ phonetically only in that one must be derived cyclically and the other not, the one which is not cyclically derived is always further in meaning from the base. This has been noted many times in the literature. We will therefore say that a word which has been in the dictionary long enough to diverge from compositionality, i.e. a word whose meaning is *no longer* derivable from that of its parts, may lose its cyclic structure. This is of course only a rough formulation. We have not said how far a word must diverge before it loses its structure, and it may be that loss of structure is an automatic consequence of loss of compositionality.

In addition, there may be other structural correlates of loss of compositionality (cf. for example the discussion of boundary strength in chapter 6). However, the statement does account for the fact that only the divergent word has no cyclic structure. It is of course an

---

[20] Within the system of Halle (1973c) the only rule which actually has the effect of subordinating stress is one which stresses a [1 stress]. The Detail Rule is such a rule. It stresses the last [1 stress] of a word, unless that stress falls on the last vowel, in which case it stresses the penult: last wins, unless it is last.

addition to our theory, which now says that though we may make up only words which are naturally bracketed, words may lose their bracketings as they go their own way. This does not seem to be a very serious addition, or to weaken our position much, and it allows us to encode very nicely the fact that only words whose meanings are not compositional will be susceptible to loss of structure, though it does not explain it. Other theories, though they allow for both cyclic and noncyclic structures, have trouble accounting for the semantic differences between the two sorts of structures in a principled way. To the extent that our present theory can accommodate the two in a principled and interesting way, it is superior.

In summary, I have shown how cyclic structures of the sort proposed by Brame arise naturally as a consequence of a theory of word-based morphology. I have also proposed a small addition to the theory which allows noncyclic structures under certain specific semantic conditions.

2.2.4.2. Irregular Back-formations. As Marchand (1969) stresses, back-formation is of diachronic relevance only. It consists of the extraction of a new word from an already existing word which appears to be bimorphemic. Within the theory just outlined it is thus just what its name says: a backwards application of a WFR. The most often quoted example of back-formation in English is the verb *peddle*, back-formed from the noun *peddler*. Historically, *peddler* is monomorphemic. However, since it is an occupational noun, and since such nouns are often formed from verbs with the suffix *-er*, the *er* became analyzed as an affix, and the stem subsequently came into use as a verb. More common in English is the borrowing of a latinate derived form, whose stem is subsequently retrieved by back-formation. Such a case is the verb *aggress*, which was back-formed from the noun *aggression*.

The fact that back-formations of any sort are possible but not necessary is easily handled in a theory in which all words in the dictionary are completely specified separate items. In other theories back-formations can be problematic. So, for example, if *aggression*, as a derived noun, is not listed in the dictionary as a completely specified form, then the form which presumably is referred to in completely specifying *aggression* at the point of lexical insertion, i.e. *aggress* must, for most speakers, be marked [*−Lexical Insertion*]. In a theory in which individual words are not independent, back-formation thus always results in a better system; in fact, the system which does not have the back-form is very bizarre. But if this is true, then why don't all speakers adopt the back-form as soon as they are exposed to it, which they do not? There are in addition problems with the notion [*−Lexical Insertion*] itself, which is so strong as to be almost vacuous. Thus the mere fact of back-formation seems to be more easily accommodated in a full-entry theory of some sort. This same point is made somewhat more forcefully by Jackendoff (1975).

However, there is real evidence that some back-forms cannot even be generated in any theory but one in which every word is a complete entry unto itself. This evidence comes from phonologically "irregular" back-forms. Consider such words as *self-destruct* and *cohese*, back-formed from *self-destruction* and *cohesion*. Within most theories, one expects the forms *self-destroy* and *cohere*, which presumably underlie the nominals and are merely marked [*−Lexical Insertion*]. The actual forms are thus impossible.

To see how they are predicted within the theory outlined so far, we must first digress a little. We have already mentioned rules of allomorphy in connection with the status of the latinate stem *mit*, and they will be discussed in detail in chapter 5. For the moment we only need to know that the morph *struct* which occurs in *self-destruction* can be an allomorph of two morphemes, one which appears word-finally as *stroy* (*destroy/destruction*) and one which appears word-finally as *struct* (*construct/construction*). The "source" of *struct/ion* is thus opaque. It could be either *struct* or *stroy*. In a full-entry theory *self-destruction* is an entity unto itself, and when we back-form from it we essentially ask ourselves, "What word *might* this one have been formed from?" We don't know and must pick the most likely one. By a principle of least effort (identical to that used in determining underlying phonological forms where the choice is indeterminate, in the theory of SPE, chapter 9) when, in the course of our "reconstruction", we arrive at a choice which is arbitrary, we choose the form which is "closest" to the one we started out from. Thus, in this instance, we must choose *struct*, which is identical, rather than *stroy*, and we arrive at the word *self-destruct* as the most likely. Within any other system, since the "source" already "exists" though it doesn't occur, we need have no recourse to any "might have been" strategy; as a result we either make the wrong prediction or can make none at all. The point is that in the full entry theory we must have a "recovery" strategy, and the most sensible recovery strategy that arises in the words-from-words hypothesis gives us exactly the right results. Our theory thus pushes us to make two decisions, both of which are vindicated by the data.

It must be stressed that within no other theory are we forced to make the right choices. A theory which does not have fully specified entries, as noted, tells us nothing about this situation. A theory which, like that of Jackendoff, has fully specified separate entries, but which relates them by redundancy rules of an arbitrary form and does not contain the notion *allomorphy rule*, tells us nothing about the proper strategy. It is only when we claim that words are formed from words by rules, each of which performs a unitary phonological operation,[21] that the proper strategy is predicted.

The same account holds for *cohese*. Since *Vs* before *+ion* can be the reflex of *Vs* (*confuse/confusion, excise/excision*), *Vd* (*delude/delusion, pervade/pervasion, provide/provision*), or *Vr* (*adhere/adhesion*), it is only by calling on the principle of least effort, and using the right strategy, that we predict *cohese*.

2.2.5. Counterevidence

Direct counterevidence to the theory that words are formed from words would be a case in which there are several words formed from the same stem, but in which the stem never shows up as a word itself. Of course, if there are only one or two such words, we might reasonably hypothesize that the nonoccurring stem has unaccountably dropped out of the language after having done its duty, or that like the case of *aggression/*aggress* we are dealing with a borrowing from a language which happens to have a similar morphology. However, when we find many

---

[21] I have not stressed the importance of this central claim. It means essentially that a rule cannot perform different operations on different stems.

stems which exhibit this peculiar phenomenon, and with the same affixes, we might reasonably hypothesize a regular rule deriving the various forms from the stems, and this would be an impossible rule in our theory. One such case is the common occurrence in English of the following paradigm:

(17)

Xion	Xive/ory	Xor	*X
incision	incisive	incisor	*incise
gustation	gustatory		*gustate
locomotion	locomotive	locomotor	*locomote
malediction	maledictory		*maledict
valediction	valedictory		*valedict
illusion	illusory		*illude
retribution	retributive/ory		*retribute
emulsion	emulsive		*emulse
revulsion	revulsive		*revulse/ *revél

The most obvious conclusion to be made from (17) is that the items *Xion*, *Xive*, *Xory*, and *Xor* are all formed from the stem *X, which, in these cases, is not an independently occurring word. However, the conclusion is contrary to the basic claim of word-based morphology and must be false if the theory is to remain.

Because of the number of cases, it is not terribly convincing to claim that they are all accidental, arising from the loss of the stem as an independently occurring item at some time after the formation of all the derivatives. This sort of thing can happen sporadically, but why should it happen so many times involving this one paradigm? Furthermore, there is evidence that some of the derivatives, at least, entered the language at a time when the stem was not an independently occurring word. Such a case is not subject to the accidental gap explanation. It would appear, then, that at least some of the words listed above constitute direct counter-examples to our theory.

Happily, this is not quite true. For reasons which are completely extraneous to ours, Martin (1972) has argued that in the above paradigm the forms *Xive*, *Xory*, and *Xor* are based on the form *Xion*. Martin's strongest evidence is that one rarely finds any of the former group occurring with stems that do not also take *-ion*, though the reverse is not true; that is, the number of words of the form *Xion* far outnumbers the total number of words ending in all the other suffixes combined.[22] This distribution only makes sense if the forms *Xive*, *Xory*, and *Xor* are derived from the forms *Xion*.

Second, when *X* does occur as an independent verb and the semantics of *X* and *Xion* do not correspond exactly, the meaning of *Xive*, etc. always corresponds to that of *Xion*. Martin's example is the set *communicate, communication, communicative*. The verb has as one of its meanings 'to receive the sacrament of *Communion*'. The noun has no corresponding meaning, and neither does the adjective. A similar example is the set *induce, induction, inductive*. In one

---

[22] Exceptions listed by Martin (1972, 6) are the following:
Xive, **Xion*: conducive, divorcive, purposive, deducive, redressive, abusive, amusive, conflictive, combative, sportive, contrastive, appointive, effective, talkative, calmative, comparative, figurative.

of its senses, the noun denotes a type of reasoning. The adjective has a corresponding sense, but the verb does not. There are many more such sets. They can be nicely accounted for if the adjective is derived from the noun or vice versa. In light of the general distribution of the two forms, i.e. the fact that there are more nouns than adjectives, the noun seems the better choice. In any case, to choose the verb or the "stem" as the base is to give up any hope of accounting for these facts.

The third piece of evidence is historical. In all the cases Martin has been able to find documentation for in the *OED*, the *-ion* form entered the language before the *-ive* form. *Exploitation* is found earlier than *exploitative*, for example. We can only make sense of these data if the *-ive* form is derived from the *-ion* form. Furthermore, the derivation must be conceived of as the addition of a newly coined word to the dictionary, something which is possible only in the sort of theory outlined in this work.

Thus we find that the seeming counterevidence to our theory is rather evidence for it. We can explain the distribution, meaning, and history of the *Xive*, *Xory*, *Xor*, and *Xion* forms only by deriving the first three from the last in the manner described by our hypothesis of word-based word formation. Though admittedly no Devil's Advocate with regard to the matter at hand, I have not found any set of data similar to (17) but not susceptible to conversion. In any case, it is clear that there is a certain sort of data which would constitute counterevidence to the claim put forth by our theory. Merely being able to determine what such data would look like demonstrates that our theory has merit as a theory. Insofar as no such data has been brought forward, and insofar as the theory sheds some light on the material which does not contradict it, it has some empirical merit.

The examples discussed in this section show another thing as well. When we speak of a word formed from another word, the simplest case will be that in which the former actually contains the latter. So [[farm]er] contains [farm]. But this will not always be true. We have evidence that *aggressive* is formed from *aggression*, yet the former does not contain the latter, on the surface at least. One never finds words of the form **Xionive*. The notion "one word formed from another" must therefore be more abstract than mere surface concatenation. This should be kept in mind.

2.2.6. Word Structure

A major fault of the theory so far delineated is that it only deals with one of the areas which are considered to be the domain of morphology. We have restricted the discussion to word formation and have disregarded the structure of already existing words.

Almost all words have morphological structure. This fact can be ascertained from the fact that the phonology must have access to both bracketing and boundaries, both of which are morphological matters. Bracketing we have discussed, and boundaries are morphologically determined to the extent that they occur between morphemes, which they almost always do. Now, from what we have said so far, it is perfectly possible that only the words a speaker actually makes up on his own will have morphological structure, and that all the other words he knows (the great majority of which he presumably learns by hearing them) have no structure. Another possibility is that the rules which determine the morphological structure of the words which a speaker does not actually make up are completely other than, and different from, the rules used to make up new words, and that the two sorts of rules just happen to produce structures of the same sort. This is possible, but highly unlikely.

We have already argued that it is reasonable to separate the rules for making up new words from those for analyzing existing words, because of the general fact that already existing words tend to be peculiar, and resistant to any system which derives their properties by general rule. This fact precludes our accounting for the similarities between word formation and word analysis in the most obvious fashion, that is, by saying they are exactly the same thing. The two matters are the same, and yet different. It would be nice if the rules governing them also had this characteristic.

We have already seen that back-formation must be a sort of unraveling of WFRs and other morphological rules (rules of allomorphy); that is, that an individual back-formation can best be viewed as the answer to the question, "What word could this one have been formed from by a regular rule?" A similar account of word structure is perfectly plausible. It would also meet the same and yet different requirement. The difference is that while the rules as rules of word formation are rules for generating forms, the same rules of word analysis can be viewed as redundancy rules. They can be used to segment a word into morphological constituents, though the word may not be strictly generable from these constituents.

There is of course little novelty in the proposal that existing morphologically complex words should be "analyzed" rather than "synthesized". Nor, once we accept the analytic position, is the use of redundancy rules a striking suggestion. It is rather perhaps the first method that comes to mind and probably the only sort that can extract anything of interest from the detritus of linguistic and social history that a lexicon presents. An extensive defense of the use of redundancy rules in morphology can be found in Jackendoff (1975). I will not repeat his points here, many of which incidentally parallel some that have been made already in this work. In addition to Jackendoff, Halle (1973a) can best be interpreted as a system of redundancy rules which extract generalizations from a dictionary.

However, the problem with these and similar systems is that they put no external constraints on the notion *redundancy rule*. Within Jackendoff's system any two facts which coincide, however incidentally, can be reduced to one. No criteria are provided for what can constitute a valid generalization. The advantage which our system enjoys over this one is the fact that the redundancy rules are defined outside the realm in which they operate: the lexicon. It is only a WFR which can serve as a redundancy rule, and WFRs are rules by which new words are formed. This means that the only sorts of facts which can count as redundancies or generalizations in the analysis of existing words are those which enter into the formation of new ones. The scope of the notion *redundancy rule* is thus automatically reduced considerably, and to a point where it embodies an interesting claim.

The analysis of a word begins at its first articulation. We have a theory which tells us what the possible parts of words are and we apply it to individual words. The noun *communalization*, formed a few pages ago, is a simple case. We recognize the suffix *+Ation* which forms abstract nouns from verbs (cf. chapter 5), the suffix #*ize* which forms verbs from adjectives, and the suffix +*al* which forms adjectives from nouns. The sum of these operations is the analysis *commune*$_N$+*al*$_A$ #*ize*$_V$ +*Ation*$_N$. In this case each step of the analysis results in a base which is a member of a lexical category, and therefore may be labeled as such.

When the analysis does not give us a base which is a member of any lexical category, then it receives no label. We can contrast in this respect the words *baker* and *butcher*, which both may be analyzed as containing the deverbal agentive suffix #*er*. The former contains a verb (*bake*), while the latter does not (**butch*$_V$). The two forms will therefore be analyzed as *bake*$_V$ #*er* and *butch*#*er* respectively. Similar to *butcher* are *possible*$_A$ and *probable*$_A$, both of which contain the deverbal adjective suffix +*abl* (cf. chapter 6) and neither of which have verbal bases; they must therefore be analyzed as *poss*+*abl*$_A$ and *prob*+*abl*$_A$.

The analysis so far is divorced from any semantic considerations. In fact, with words like *probable* and *butcher*, there will be no semantics, for there is no base on which the semantic function may operate. We cannot ask whether the meaning of the whole is a function of the independently established meaning of its parts, because one of its parts has no independent meaning. This is as it should be. Clearly, there is a difference in the arbitrariness of *probable* and *bad*. The former contains a suffix which is a common marker of its lexical category; +*abl* reduces the arbitrariness of *probable*'s being an adjective. The latter contains no such redundant information. But this is as far as it goes. We know more about *probable* than about *bad*, but not much more.[23]

When a word does have a base, it is legitimate to ask about the semantic relationship between the two. Since morphology is not syntax, this relationship will seldom be one of neat compositionality. There will usually be some sort of divergence. Intuitively, this divergence is not between the derivative and the base, but rather between the actual meaning of the derivative and the meaning we expect it to have, given the independently occurring meaning of the base. So, for example, the divergence of *transmission* (of a car) consists in the fact that it does not mean 'action of transmitting'. The divergence is therefore not directly between *transmission*

---

[23] Note that to label *prob* as a verb and then mark it as (for some reason) nonoccurring would be to claim that *probable* has all and only the properties which +*abl* assigns. That claim is quickly shown to be false. A curious syntactic property of productively derived words, first noted by Ross (1974), is that they tend to be more limited in their subcategorizations than other words. In the case at hand, we find that when a verb allows either sentential *that* -clause or nominal objects, its +*abl* derivative allows only the nominal:

    (i)   We determined that the butler had done it.
    (ii)   We determined the exact nature of the substance.
    (iii) The exact nature of the substance is not determinable.
    (iv) *That the butler had done it was not determinable.
    (v)   *It was not determinable that the butler had done it.

If *possible* were indeed derived from **poss*$_V$, we would expect to find a corresponding pattern of grammaticality, which we do not:

    (vi) That the butler had done it was possible.
    (vii) It was possible that the butler had done it.

The same is true of *probable*.

It is evident from this and similar examples that the analysis of words is not a synthetic procedure, but rather merely a method of extracting redundancies.

and *transmit*, but rather between the two senses of *transmission*. The expected sense of the derivative thus mediates between its actual sense and the actual sense of the base. This intuitive notion of divergence is the one most easily handled in our theory. Since the anlysis outlined so far concerns only the form of a word, we are now free to give this analyzed form a putative meaning by applying the compositional semantic functions of any affixes it may contain to the base. As an example consider the word *information*. Disregarding the semantics, we give it the analysis $inform_V + Ation_N$. We then give this form a meaning, approximately 'act(ion) of informing' or 'event or state of being informed'. We next compare this meaning with the meanings of *information* which we determine from its actual use in the language. As it happens, only one of these comes close, the one exemplified in the following sentence:

(18) The function of a public library is information.

In a fully developed theory of semantics, there will be some method for quantifying this divergence and perhaps even some notion of "possible divergence".[24] I will not provide such a theory or such a method, but merely wish to point out that the function to be computed and the elements on which it depends are all natural consequences of our theory of word analysis and, furthermore, make sense.

Note that a central claim of this approach to the analysis of existing words is that relatedness of form is prior to relatedness of meaning in morphology. There are cases in which we can define only formal relationships, as with *possible*, but in no case are we able to define only semantic relationships. Semantics is not irrelevant, but rather cannot be called into play until we have laid the formal foundation. Among other things, this means that synonymy is excluded from the purview of derivational morphology.

Our system of word analysis will handle the two different types of berries discussed in 2.1. A word like *cranberry* will be treated in a fashion exactly parallel to *possible*. Thus, in our system, we can account for what we know about a partially motivated form without having it collapse with completely motivated ones. Since we know what *berry* is likely to mean, we have some idea as to a possible meaning for *cranberry*. However, since *cran* occurs nowhere in our system of rules and words, we have no way even to guess at the complete meaning of the entire word. *Blueberry* can be segmented into otherwise occurring parts. However, there are very few parts of the meaning of *blueberry* that are not attributable to the berry compound form and that are shared with other meanings of *blue*. *Blueberry* will thus be very distant from *blue*, which I think is the correct view of the mannner and closeness of the relation between the two. Note that we do not run into any problems with regard to *blue* as a partially meaningful element in *blueberry*. We are concerned with the meaning of the entire word. The fact that *blue* occurs as an independent word is of interest and demands that we compare that word with *blueberry*, but not with the morpheme *blue* which is part of that word. This is not a sophistic point.[25]

---

[24] Vergnaud (1973) develops in some detail one general type of system by which such a quantification may be accomplished. Ullman (1962) provides a traditional and enlightening account of the problems involved.

[25] For more on the treatment of partially motivated forms within a system like the one proposed, see Jackendoff (1975).

Viewing word analysis as a backwards sort of word formation thus has virtues apart from its nice compatibility with our system. It allows us to account for what we know from general principles and to separate this from what is either not included in or counter to such general principles.

I will not dwell any further on existing words. Except for the few points mentioned here, the rules for analyzing words are essentially degenerate versions of the rules for forming new ones. One might wish to speculate on the nature of the degeneration, but in order to be able to do so we must first gain some knowledge of the nature of the healthy specimens. Chapter 4 represents a few first steps in this direction.

3: Productivity

We turn in this chapter to a discussion of the notion of *productivity*. The turning will seem abrupt to some, for up to this point the matter has hardly been mentioned. Yet productivity is one of the central mysteries of derivational morphology. It is the root of the strange and persistent fact that, though many things are possible in morphology, some are more possible than others.

The term *productivity* is widely used in studies of derivational morphology, and there is obviously some intuition behind the usage, but most of the discussion of it is rather vague. Indeed, mere mention of the subject seems to be taken by many as an open invitation to anecdotalism. In what is perhaps a reaction to tradition, I have attempted to restrict my own discussion to very specific properties, properties which seem to characteristically distinguish productive from nonproductive WFRs. The discussion will be imbedded in a comparison of the two English nominal affixes #*ness* and +*ity* in one particular morphological environment: when they are attached to adjectives of the form *Xous*. The framework of the analysis will be that of chapter 2. In fact, the entire method of the present chapter presupposes that of the last: much of what will be said simply makes little or no sense in other systems. Therefore, any credit which this discussion of productivity may enjoy must redound to its predecessor. First, however, some preliminaries.

3.1. Preliminaries

It is sometimes claimed that productivity is a matter which never enters into the study of syntax. This is not quite true. Compare the two rules Dative Movement and Passive. Observe, in the case of the former, that the predicates which permit it, while members of a more or less well-defined semantic class, are not all the members of that class, but rather some reasonably arbitrary selection of them. On the other hand, while there are some transitive verbs which do not allow Passive, the exceptions seem to be principled. One would appear to be justified, therefore, in saying that Passive is more productive than Dative Movement.[1] Of course, in syntax there are certain types of operations which are immune to questions of productivity. Such rules as Subject-Auxiliary Inversion, which are not optional in any sense of the term, cannot ever be thought of in terms of productivity. In contrast, WFRs are always optional.

---

[1] A more detailed discussion of this question is presented in Oehrle (1975).

A first attempt to articulate one's intuitions about the meaning and utility of the term *productivity* in morphology generally identifies productivity with sheer number. If we want to compare the productivity of two WFRs, we may simply make lists of the words formed by the respective processes and add them up. The longer the list, the more productive the WFR. An immediate objection to this method, however, is that it isn't fair: it doesn't take into account the fact that there are morphological restrictions on the sorts of words one may use as the base of certain WFRs. Thus, #*ment* and +*ion* both form nouns from verbs (*detachment, inversion*), but the latter is restricted to latinate verbs. There is a simple way to take such restrictions into account: we count up the number of words which we feel *could* occur as the output of a given WFR (which we can do by counting the number of possible bases for the rule), count up the number of actually occurring words formed by that rule, take a ratio of the two, and compare this with the same ratio for another WFR. In fact, by this method we could arrive at a simple index of productivity for every WFR: the ratio of possible to actually listed words.

Two problems face this simple method. The first is not crucial, but often overlooked in more cursory discussions of productivity (not, however, in many traditional accounts). It is simply that one cannot speak absolutely about the productivity of a WFR. Rather, one must ask how productive an affix is when attached to words of a particular morphological class.[2] Thus, compare the two affixes #*ness* and +*ity* when attached to two distinct classes of base adjectives, those ending in *ive* (*perceptive*) and those ending in *ile* (*servile*). The simple list tells us that #*ness* is more productive than +*ity* with the former class of bases (Walker (1936) lists approximately five times the number of words of the form *Xiveness* as those of the form *Xivity*). However, this result does not carry over to the second class of bases. The number of words of the form *Xility* overwhelmingly exceeds that of those of the form *Xileness*. In the one case one affix is more productive, in the other case the other is. Thus, there is no absolute way to say that one WFR is more productive than another. Rather, one must take into account the morphology of the base.[3]

The second problem with the simple mechanical method of computing productivity is that it depends very crucially on the idea that every time we make up a new word, it is entered in a list. Unless all new words are listed, we have no effective procedure for computing the ratio of existing to possible words, even when we restrict ourselves to a particular morphological class of bases, and hence no effective way of computing an index of productivity. With some very productive WFRs, the notion of a list is simply counterintuitive. For example, the adverb-forming suffix -*ly*, which is far and away the most productive WFR in English, occupies some 34 pages in Walker's dictionary, many more than any other affix. But when we glance at this

---

[2] One modern author who does stress the fact that morphological form affects productivity is Karl Zimmer (1964), especially in his discussion of the productivity of the negative prefix *un#* with bases which are past participles or adjectives of the form *Xable* as opposed to monomorphemic adjectives.

[3] There is still a valid sense of the general productivity of a WFR. A WFR whose general productivity is high will have few morphological restrictions on the class of bases to which it attaches. Thus, +*ity*, while it may be very productive with certain limited morphological classes of adjectives, does not extend its domain to new morphological classes, while #*ness* is fairly free morphologically. The general productivity of #*ness* is therefore higher. But this matter is entirely separate from the one under discussion in this chapter.

list, we feel somehow that it is superfluous. With such a productive rule as this it seems sufficient just to take an adjective – almost any English adjective[4] – and tack on *-ly* to make an adverb.

Later in this chapter I will present some concrete, and I think convincing, evidence that the output of the most productive WFRs does not meet independently established criteria for listing. There are good reasons for not listing all the *-ly* adverbs in English. This means that there is no procedure for computing productivity from mere numbers, but rather that the productivity of a WFR is the result of the interplay of a complex of factors, some of which I have attempted to isolate.

One more point must be made before proceeding: speakers of a language have intuitions about productivity. I will give an example of what I mean by this. Consider again the two suffixes *#ness* and *+ity* attached to bases of the form *Xive*. Take one word out of the class *Xive*, *perceptive*, and form with the suffixes the two words *perceptiveness* and *perceptivity*. Present these two words to native speakers of English and they will almost invariably say that though both words are possible, one of them, *perceptiveness*, sounds "better". *Perceptivity* is said to be "awkward" or "fancy". The same will hold for any other pair of words of the form *Xiveness* and *Xivity*, provided that neither is an already common word. Clearly, speakers are not using lists when they give these answers; rather, they are showing evidence of having direct access to an intuition. This intuition seems to express the notion "likelihood of being a word of the speaker's active vocabulary", a notion equivalent to productivity. Of course we are not interested merely in the existence of the intuition, nor even in how the speaker provides it (that is much too large a task). Rather we would like to explore some of its more objective correlates and the factors which determine it.

3.2. *#ness* and *+ity*

Our method of investigation will be to compare in some detail two WFRs which we know to differ in productivity. In order to isolate productivity, we try to choose rules which come as close as possible to differing only in that dimension, thus removing outside factors which might interfere with our results. We therefore must take two rules which operate on the same base and have outputs of the same lexical category and subcategorization. Such rival pairs are not easy to come by, for morphological restrictions are often arranged so as to preclude them. The most interesting pair is probably *+abl* and *#abl*, which we will discuss in some detail in chapter 6, but the mere justification of the distinction between the two is a long matter, and we will turn instead to that reliable standard example, the pair *#ness* and *+ity*, both of which form abstract nouns from adjectives. One of the largest morphological subclasses of adjectives in which they clash is that of the form *Xous* (*monstrous*), and we will select this as our base.

It is clear that *#ness* attaches more productively to bases of the form *Xous* than does *+ity*: *fabulousness* is much "better" than *fabulosity*, and similarly for other pairs (*dubiousness/ dubiety, dubiosity*). There are even cases where the *+ity* derivative is not merely worse, but

---

[4] Systematically, *-ly* does not attach to adjectives which themselves end in *-ly* (*silly/*sillily*). *ly* will also not attach to an adjective which already has an adverb associated with it (*good/well/*goodly*$_{\text{Adv}}$).

impossible. *acrimonious/*acrimoniosity, euphonious/*euphoniosity, famous/*famosity*. There is also the simple list test, which is still a good indicator. Walker (1936) lists fewer +*ity* derivatives than #*ness* derivatives of words of the form *Xous*.

3.2.1. Semantics

An important difference between the two sets is that the semantics of *Xousness* is more *coherent*. We say that a WFR is coherent when the words formed by that rule adhere closely to the meaning assigned to them by the semantic function of the rule. Put another way, a WFR is coherent to the extent that one can predict the meaning of any word formed by that rule.

All nouns of the form *Xousness* have the following three paraphrases:[5]

  a. '*the fact that Y is Xous*'
     His callousness surprised me. = The fact that he was callous surprised me.
  b. '*the extent to which Y is Xous*'
     His callousness surprised me. = The extent to which he was callous surprised me.
  c. '*the quality or state of being Xous*'
     Callousness is not a virtue. = The quality or state of being callous is not a virtue.

Furthermore, nouns of the form *Xousness* do not have other meanings. It is thus possible to predict that any noun of this form will have all and only the meanings paraphrased by (a), (b), and (c). The class is therefore semantically completely coherent.

The semantics of the +*ity* derivatives is not nearly so coherent. Though many have the three readings (a), (b), and (c), some lack one or more of these. There are also sometimes other readings: technical senses, concrete nouns, count nouns. Finally, nouns of this class appear more readily in idiomatic contexts. I will give a number of examples. In each case, (a), (b), or (c) is placed before sentences in which the +*ity* derivative has the appropriate reading. *Other* is prefaced in all instances where the reading is different from the three usual ones.

(1) *Readings of* +ity *Nouns*
   (i) *various/variety*
      a, b) The variety of the fish in the pond surprised me.
         c) Variety is not always pleasing.
      other) How many varieties of fish are there in the pond?
   (ii) *notorious/notoriety*
      a, b) His notoriety appealed to me.
         c) Notoriety is not a virtue.
      other) All the town's notables and notorieties were there.
   (iii) *curious/curiosity*
      a, b) His curiosity disturbed me.
         c) Curiosity can be dangerous.
      other) They admired his dress, but only as a curiosity.

---

[5] It is not clear that we are dealing with three separate readings rather than one tripartite or ambiguous one. I lean towards the latter, but due to the present state of the art of semantics, and perhaps to my own incompetence, I will leave this very interesting question open.

(iv) *porous/porosity*
   a, b) The porosity of the material is uncanny.
   c) Porosity is often a highly desired quality.
   other) The high porosity (*porousness) of the clay made it unfit for use.
(v) *monstrous/monstrosity*
   a, b) The monstrosity of what I had done suddenly dawned upon me.
   c) ??Monstrosity is not a pleasant quality.
   other) What a monstrosity!
(vi) *continuous/continuity*
   a, b) The continuity of one's heritage can be disturbing.
   other) This story lacks continuity.
      The continuities for next week's episode.
(vii) *discontinuous/discontinuity*
   ? a) There is a sense of discontinuity, failure to follow through.
   other) There are many discontinuities in your story.

We can find striking confirmation of the difference in coherence between +*ity* and #*ness* by comparing the derivatives of negative and positive adjectives. Thus, compare *continuity* and *discontinuity* with their counterparts *continuousness* and *discontinuousness*. The latter differ only to the extent that their bases do, something which can hardly be said of the former. The difference may be expressed proportionally:

(2) *continuous:discontinuous = continuousness:discontinuousness*
    continuous:discontinuous ≠ continuity:discontinuity

As far as I can tell, there is a direct link between semantic coherence and productivity. Zimmer (1964) has investigated in some detail the English negative prefixes *un#* and *non#* as well as similar negative affixes in other languages. He has found that where an affix is productive its semantics is, in our terms, coherent: "Where one is dealing with a clearly productive morphological process, a simple statement of the semantic content of the process in question ...seems to be as much as can or should be expected..." (Zimmer (1964, 32)).[6] Another somewhat detailed example is found in chapter 6 of this monograph, where the English suffixes #*abl* and +*abl* are discussed. The former is found to be more productive and more coherent.

If we can accept them, the value judgments of speakers also agree with the linking of productivity and coherence, for speakers will usually say of the "less likely" member of a pair such as *connectiveness/connectivity* that it "should have a special sense". Commonsensically, the correlation is perfectly reasonable: the surer one is of what a word will mean, the more likely one is to use it.

---

[6] A particularly nice observation of Zimmer's is that there is a correlation of productivity with contrary vs. contradictory negation. When a negation rule is productive, its output is contradictory of the base (*not X*, where *X* is the base), whereas when the rule is less productive, its output is contrary (*no X*, or *opposite to X*). The following pairs are well-known examples of this phenomenon:

non-Christian (contradictory):unchristian (contrary)
nonhuman (contradictory):inhuman (contrary)

3.2.2. Phonology

The two suffixes #*ness* and +*ity* differ in the manner of their attachment. #*ness* attaches with a word boundary, represented by #, while +*ity* attaches with a morpheme boundary, represented by +. These boundaries were introduced into linguistics by Chomsky and Halle. Their actual nature is discussed in chapters 4 and 6, and in Siegel (1974). The net phonological effect of the difference between + and # is that on the phonetic surface the segmental phonology and stress of *Xous* are the same in both *Xous* and *Xousness*, whereas with +*ity* stress shifts to the syllable preceding the affix (*luminous/luminosity*) and this syllable is always lax, due to the effect of the rule of *trisyllabic shortening*[7] (*mendacious/mendacity*). The + boundary suffix thus makes the derived word phonetically further from the base. This fact is not, however, always relevant to questions of productivity.[8]

One curious fact about the phonology of +*ity* is that its attachment sometimes triggers the loss of the *ous* which precedes it: *simultaneous/simultaneity/*simultaneosity, voracious/voracity/*voraciosity*. Formally, we may represent the process as *R1*:

R1. (ous *Truncation*)
os → φ / ___ +ity

A rule like this, which deletes the last morpheme of a base before a suffix, is called a rule of *truncation*. (The general phenomenon of truncation is quite common and will be discussed at length in chapter 5.) For example, +*ate* drops regularly before +*ant* (*continue/continuant, operate/operant/*operatant*). R1 is unusual, though, in that it does not take place in all the words which meet the conditions for it. Thus we have *various/variety*, but *curious/curiosity*; similarly *sedulous/sedulity*, but *fabulous/fabulosity*. Nor do we find any free variation in individual words: for a given base, R1 will either always or never apply. Neither **curiety* nor **variosity* is ever found.

Odder still is the fact that in the large majority of cases it is impossible to predict from any general property of a word whether it will undergo R1 or not. *Curious* and *various* are very close phonologically, as are *sedulous* and *fabulous*. Thus, the application of R1 is determined by individual words; it is *lexically governed*.

The lexical government of R1 has a great effect on the productivity of +*ity*.[9] Evidence for this assertion is the fact that when R1 is governed not by the individual word but by a more general factor, the number of +*ity* derivatives increases markedly, which is to say that the productivity of +*ity* increases.

---

[7] This rule basically shortens the vowel of any stressed syllable which is three or more syllables from the end of a word. It is discussed at length in SPE.

[8] There is a sense in which # is stronger than +. The strength of a boundary is reflected in the semantic compositionality of the word formed by its bond. As Shelvador (1974) points out, whenever two words differ solely in the strength of an internal boundary, the one with the stronger boundary is closer to compositionality (*cónference/conférence*). Boundary strength is discussed below in chapter 6. However, it is not always true that WFRs with weak boundaries are not productive. +*Ation*, for example, is very productive with bases of the form *Xize* (cf. chapter 5).

[9] The more globally minded might take heart at finding that although R1 intrinsically follows +*ity* attachment, its operation affects that of the earlier rule. Note, however, that it is the lexical marking for R1 which is the culprit, rather than R1 itself.

PRODUCTIVITY

We will compare the +*ity* derivatives of words of the classes *XVcious* (*mendacious*) and *Xulous* (*bibulous*). With the first class of bases the application of R1 is not governed by the individual word but rather by the vowel which precedes *ci*:

(3) Xacious   Xacity   *Xaciosity
     (mordacious)   (mordacity)   (*mordaciosity)

     Xocious   Xocity   *Xociosity
     (precocious)   (precocity)   (*precociosity)

     Xecious   *Xecity   Xeciosity
     (specious)   (*specity)   (speciosity)

The rule documented in (3) is that if the conditioning vowel is *a* or *o*, then R1 applies, but if the vowel is *e*, then R1 does not apply.[10] All words follow this rule; there are no exceptions. In contrast, the class *Xulous* observes no such general rule:

(4) nebulous   *nebulity   nebulosity
     credulous   credulity   *credulosity

Since the operation of R1 is lexically governed in +*ity* derivatives of words of the class *Xulous* and is not lexically governed in +*ity* derivatives of words of the class *XVcious*, we expect +*ity* to be more productive with the latter base than with the former. To test this prediction, we will compare the lists in Walker (1936) of the following four classes: *Xacious, Xacity, Xulous, Xulosity/Xulity*. These are given in the following tables:[11]

(5) bibacious   *   pugnacious   pugnacity
     efficacious   *   pertinacious   pertinacity
     inefficacious *   minacious   minacity
     perspicacious perspicacity   capacious   capacity
     pervicacious   pervicacity   rapacious   rapacity
     procacious   procacity   spacious   *
     edacious   edacity   feracious   feracity
     mendacious   mendacity   veracious   veracity
     mordacious   mordacity   gracious   *
     audacious   audacity   voracious   voracity
     sagacious   sagacity   vivacious   vivacity
     fugacious   fugacity   sequacious   *
     salacious   salacity   loquacious   loquacity
     tenacious   tenacity
     fumacious   *
     contumacious   *

[10] Exactly what sort of conditioning factor is at work here is not clear to me. Strictly speaking, it is phonological, but the quality of the vowel in such a position does not strike me as a particularly natural phonological condition for a rule such as R1.

[11] We do not include the classes *Xocious* and *Xecious* and their derivatives since these classes are too small to be of real value.

(6)
fabulous	fabulosity	glandulous	*
sebulous	*	pendulous	*
nebulous	nebulosity	undulous	*
noctambulous	*	nodulous	*
bibulous	*	scrofulous	*
tubulous	*	solidungulous	*
miraculous	*	orgulous	*
craculous	*	cellulous	cellulosity
flocculous	*	ramulous	*
pediculous	*	emulous	*
ridiculous	*	tremulous	*
folliculous	*	cumulous	*
vermiculous	*	granulous	*
ventriculous	*	crapulous	*
meticulous	*	populous	*
calculous	*	scrupulous	scrupulosity
loculous	*	unscrupulous	*
monoculous	*	scaberulous	*
tuberculous	*	querulous	*
flosculous	*	torulous	*
credulous	credulity	garrulous	garrulity
incredulous	incredulity	patulous	*
sedulous	sedulity	edentulous	*
acidulous	*	tortulous	*
rigidulous	*	fistulous	*
stridulous	*	pustulous	*

The data is very clearly in accord with our prediction. There are 29 adjectives of the form *Xacious*. All but 8 of these have corresponding nominals of the form *Xacity*. There are 52 adjectives of the form *Xulous*. Only 8 of these have corresponding nominals. We see that when there is a condition on the application of R1 which is not lexically determined, there are very few gaps in the +*ity* paradigm. On the contrary, where we have no such general condition, we have many gaps and in fact very few actually occurring nominals.

The connection between lexical marking and lack of productivity is not surprising when we look at the matter from a broader, social perspective. A speaker confronted with an adjective of the form *Xacious*, from which he wishes to form a nominal in +*ity*, will know that the nominal must be *Xacity* and will, therefore, not hesitate to use it. When faced, however, with an adjective in *Xulous*, he is in a quandary. Which is correct, *Xulity* or *Xulosity*? He doesn't know, though he does know that one of the forms is correct, that there is no free variation. In order to avoid the stigma of using the wrong word, he simply uses neither and falls back on the trusty *Xness* form, where he knows that though he is surely revealing the paucity of his vocabulary, he cannot make a mistake. Thus, on very general social grounds, we can see a direct connection between the condition on R1 and the mere use of the form in +*ity*. When the former is more general, the latter is more likely to be used. It should be noted that with #*ness*, which is generally more productive than +*ity*, there is no rule corresponding to R1 and hence no need for any lexical marking at all. It is reasonable to conjecture that this fact in some way contributes to the greater productivity of #*ness*.

3.2.3. Lexical Government and the Lexicon

What does it mean for a rule to be lexically governed? Most importantly, every word which might undergo the lexically governed rule must bear an arbitrary marker, in this case either +R1 or −R1.[12] This means that all such words must be entered in a list to which we can refer. What is this list? The most obvious candidate is the lexicon. The lexicon is conventionally viewed as the repository of all the arbitrary items of a grammar (cf. Chomsky (1965) and Bloomfield (1933)), and within our framework these exceptional items will for the most part be (derivational) words. Let us say that all and *only* those words which are exceptional, i.e. arbitrary in at least one of their various features, will be entered in the lexicon. From this definition it follows that the +*ity* derivatives of most *Xous* adjectives must be entered in the lexicon. It also follows that the #*ness* derivatives, unless they are exceptional in some way which we have yet to discover, *must not* be listed in the lexicon.

It is easy to see how listing in the lexicon can affect semantic coherence. We have assumed that the mere fact that a word persists is the main root of its semantic wanderings. We now admit that the +*ity* derivatives of adjectives of the form *Xous* must be listed in the lexicon. The reason for this is not semantic. However, it is evident that the first condition for semantic drift is now met: mere persistence. Note that with the small subclass of *Xous* adjectives where the marking is not arbitrary, those of the form *XVcious*, there is no need to enter individual derivatives in the lexicon, and hence no expectation that they will drift. This expectation is borne out by the data. A short perusal of the nouns in (5) shows that they are semantically coherent, and in accord with the general meaning for deadjectival abstract nouns.

Seen as a result of listing, semantic drift might itself undermine the productivity of the WFR whose derivatives must be listed. Once a class's semantics has become incoherent through semantic drift, we run into the same practical problem we faced concerning its form. Assuming of course that the meaning of an affix is connected somehow with its distribution, with its meaning in individual forms, our ability to predict the meaning of a new form will be impaired by the arbitrary meanings of the existing listed forms. Thus, listing may affect productivity through a semantic connection.

However, there is a more direct connection between lexical listing and productivity. The key to this connection is a phenomenon which I call *blocking*. *Blocking* is the nonoccurrence of one form due to the simple existence of another. In the case at hand, we find that whenever there exist in a given stem both an adjective of the form *Xous* and a semantically related abstract noun, then it is not possible to form the +*ity* derivative of the *Xous* adjective. The

---

[12] As with two-vowel languages, we could always reduce the number of marks by a simple redundancy rule, removing all instances of −R1 and restoring them by convention. Such a device merely masks the real situation, however, for neither + nor − is in any sense less marked here.

already existing noun blocks the new +ity derivative.[13] #ness derivatives of Xous adjectives are never blocked. The pattern is exemplified in (7):

(7)
Xous	Nominal	+ity	#ness
various	*	variety	variousness
curious	*	curiosity	curiousness
glorious	glory	*gloriosity	gloriousness
furious	fury	*furiosity	furiousness
specious	*	speciosity	speciousness
precious	*	preciosity	preciousness
gracious	grace	*graciosity	graciousness
spacious	space	*spaciosity	spaciousness
tenacious	*	tenacity	tenaciousness
fallacious	fallacy	*fallacity	fallaciousness
acrimonious	acrimony	*acrimoniosity	acrimoniousness
impecunious	*	impecuniosity	impecuniousness
laborious	labor	*laboriosity	laboriousness
bilious	bile	*biliosity	biliousness
pious	*	piety	piousness

[13] The blocking abstract noun is usually the base of the *Xous* adjective. Sometimes this fact is transparent:

(i)
melody	melodious
felony	felonious
glory	glorious
hazard	hazardous
outrage	outrageous
scandal	scandalous
trouble	troublous
libel	libelous
fame	famous
venom	venomous

Sometimes there is truncation of the base-final *y*:

(ii)
synonymy	synonymous
monotony	monotonous
larceny	larcenous
homophony	homophonous
mutiny	mutinous
felicity	felicitous

A more unusual form of truncation is found below:

(iii)
quotation	quotatious
disputation	disputatious
repetition	repetitious
contradiction	contradictious
caution	cautious
pretention	pretentious
deception	deceptious
superstition	superstitious

Note that *Xion* cannot be derived from *Xious* since there is already good evidence in many cases that *Xion* is derived from the verb: *deceive/deception*, *flirt/flirtation*. More on *Xion* can be found in chapter 5.

We can account for the distribution in (7) simply by appealing to the fact that +*ity* derivatives of *Xous* adjectives must be listed in the lexicon. We may assume that the lexicon is arranged according to stems, and that for each stem there is a slot for each canonical meaning, where "canonical" means derived by regular rules (we will say more about the semantics of WFRs in chapter 4). Let us furthermore assume that for each stem there cannot be more than one item in each meaning slot. If the +*ity* nominals are entered in the lexicon, then when we make up such a form we put it into the slot for abstract nominal for its stem. However, when there is already a nominal in the stem in question, then there is no room for the +*ity* nominal; it is blocked by the already occurring nominal. When there is no nominal in that stem, then we are free to insert the +*ity* form, though, as we have already noted, this will not always happen. Thus the mere fact that the +*ity* nominals must be listed accounts neatly for the distribution of most of the forms of (7).

What about the #*ness* forms, however? Why are they not blocked? The answer to this is straightforward: we have found no reason to list them. On the assumption that only words which are arbitrary in some way must be entered in the lexicon, there is no reason to enter the #*ness* derivatives of *Xous* adjectives in the lexicon. The most productive classes never have to be listed.[14] If the #*ness* forms are never listed, then they can never be blocked, and this is what we find. Nor will there be any sporadic gaps, since the concept of gap presupposes a list, and we have no list. Nor will they drift semantically, since on our account semantic drift itself presupposes that the item which drifts be listed in the lexicon.

The pattern which emerges from (7) can be systematically attributed to whether or not a new word is listed in the lexicon. The words which must be listed are blocked, and those which must not be listed are not blocked. The pattern thus directly supports our criterion for lexical listing. Less directly, it shows, like (5) and (6), the effect of phonological factors on productivity. That there should be such effects is interesting, for it brings out the remarkable interdependence of the various subsystems of language, an interdependence which is often ignored in analyses which are restricted to only one vantage point.

3.3. Conclusions

Several points emerge from our analysis. First, productivity goes hand in hand with semantic coherence. However, we have no real evidence as to which of these is primary, or even as to whether they are really distinct matters. The second point concerns the relationship between lexical listing and productivity. Here a simple sort of causality emerges. The listing of the output of a WFR in the lexicon leads to a loss in productivity. Almost incidentally, this second point answers a question posed at the very beginning of the chapter: Are all new words entered in the lexicon? The answer is no.

There is clearly much more work to be done here. We cannot claim to have discovered in these few pages all that there is to know about productivity. Some of the ideas have only been tentatively established, though I believe they point in the right direction. Yet, what has been said does rest on a concrete basis, and that is a step forward.

---

[14] To my knowledge, Zimmer was the first person to suggest that productive and nonproductive classes could be distinguished by claiming that only members of the latter were listed in the lexicon.

4: Word Formation Rules

Merely to say that words are formed from words is neither novel nor enlightening. To make the statement interesting, we must be able to make more precise claims about the nature of the rules which generate words, their form, the conditions under which they operate, and their relation to the rest of the grammar. The elaboration of such claims is the task of this chapter.

A basic assumption we will be making is that WFRs are rules of the lexicon, and as such operate totally within the lexicon. They are totally separate from the other rules of the grammar, though not from the other components of the grammar. A WFR may make reference to syntactic, semantic, and phonological properties of words, but not to syntactic, semantic, or phonological rules. Nor may a WFR refer to those properties of words which are directly associated with these rules, i.e. such properties as syntactic or phonological rule features. This is not a strange assumption. Though it is not controversial to allow a phonological rule to refer to the fact that a certain item is a verb, for example, one does not allow such a rule to refer to the fact that it is a verb that does not undergo the Passive rule. We will assume that a WFR, as well as not referring to other types of rules and related matters, cannot introduce rule-conditioned properties. This assumption is stronger than the last, and it will be discussed below. It is tied in with two earlier assumptions: that a WFR and its associated phonological operation are one and simultaneous; and that, as a consequence, words are entered in the lexicon in a fully concrete, specified form. A related assumption is that WFRs are different from other rules in the manner and occasion of their use. The syntactic and phonological rules are necessary and essential to the generation of every sentence. It is impossible to speak without using some analogue of the syntax and the phonology. However, this is not the case with the rules of the morphology. It is the dictionary entries themselves which are the input to the syntax and phonology, and the WFRs are merely rules for adding to and, derivatively, analyzing, these entries. Thus it is very easy to speak a sentence without having any recourse to these rules. They are not "on line". Though this fact does not necessarily mean that WFRs will differ from others in their formal properties, it does suggest that the two categories are quite separate.

For every WFR we must know two basic sorts of things. First, we must know what sort of information a WFR can have access to, and how it has access to this information. It is obvious that every WFR may have access to its base, i.e. the class of words on which it operates, and to the information contained in its base. It is also possible that a WFR can take into account information other than that contained in the base. It might have access to its own output, or to forms related to the base. However, access to anything other than the base calls for rules of a much more powerful sort than we would prefer to have. We will therefore operate on the assumption that a WFR can be cognizant only of information contained in its own base.

The second sort of thing one must know about is the sorts of operations a WFR performs, the sorts of changes it can make, and the formal mechanism by which these changes can best be stated in a general way.

Perpendicular to this classification of phenomena there lies another. There are different kinds of information in a grammar: syntactic, semantic, phonological, and morphological. Words contain information of all these types, and WFRs, as rules for making up new words, most likely introduce all of these types of information as well. This chapter will be organized along this latter axis. First we will discuss the syntax and semantics of WFRs, then their morphology, and finally their phonology. Under each of these headings we will discuss first phenomena relating to the base, then phenomena relating to the output and operation of the rules. Finally, we will attempt to synthesize from all these data a description of the general properties of WFRs.[1]

4.1. Syntax and Semantics

4.1.1. The Base and the Unitary Base Hypothesis

The base is always specified syntactically. So, for example, the rule which attaches the suffix #*ness* (*redness, porousness*) operates only on adjectives. Finer syntactic distinctions than the merely categorial are possible, and matters of subcategorization are commonly referred to. Thus, the suffix +*ee* (cf. Siegel (1971)) attaches only to transitive verbs (*employee, payee, *travelee*). WFRs may also be sensitive to the selectional restrictions of the base. So, this same suffix is further restricted to verbs which allow animate objects or indirect objects (*tearee*). More detailed, and a little more exotic, is the constraint on the base for the prefix *re*#, which forms words such as *repaint* and *rewire*[2] and which has been studied in some detail by Williams (1973). This prefix attaches only to verbs whose meanings entail a change of state, generally in the object of the verb. Compare the following sentences:

(1) John punched Bill.

(2) *John repunched Bill.

(3) John punched the holes in the paper.

(4) John repunched the holes in the paper.

---

[1] This chapter is of necessity at once more programmatic and more detailed than the others in this book. We know that there are WFRs in a grammar and we have some very general ideas about these objects. Now our task is to be specific. We must therefore look at many WFRs and examine their intricacies. This makes for detail. At the same time, since the framework is new, we are less certain than we might be of individual analyses and their import. The combination sometimes leads to a form of exposition disconcertingly characteristic of the field: the baroque maelstrom, wherein the import of a given argument seems to be directly correlated with its distance from the apparently major aspects of an analysis and wherein the answer is so far from the question as to destroy any link between the two. I have tried to avoid this Charybdis.

[2] We are discussing here the prefix *re*#, which is distinct from the prefix *re*= of *refer* and the prefix *re*+ of *remind*. The distinction between # and + is more than phonological and is treated in some detail in chapter 6.

The grammaticality of (4) and the corresponding ungrammaticality of (2) can be accounted for by the above-mentioned constraint on the meaning of the base. The verb *punch* of (1) does not entail any change of state in its object. I may punch someone without my action having any effect on the person. There is no change of state; therefore, *re#* is not possible and we judge (2) to be ungrammatical. On the other hand, the verb *punch* of (3) does imply a change of state in its object. If I punch a hole in something, the object punched has been perceptibly changed; therefore, *re#* is possible with this verb, and (4) is a good sentence.

It appears to be a general fact that the syntactic and semantic conditions on the base of a WFR are those of category, subcategory, selection, and lexically governed entailment and presupposition. These are the same sorts of restriction that are relevant to lexical insertion. Note that there is, to my knowledge, no correspondence between the conditions on WFRs and those on transformations other than lexical insertion. For example, the base of a WFR never need contain a variable. This fact strengthens the assertion of Chomsky (1970) that WFRs are very different rules from syntactic transformations.

We will assume that the syntacticosemantic specification of the base, though it may be more or less complex, is always unique. A WFR will never operate on either this or that. The seeming counterexamples to this that I have found can be analyzed as separate rules whose operations happen to be homophonous. Consider the affix *#able*, which attaches to both nouns (*fashionable, sizable*) and verbs (*acceptable, doable*). The most concrete evidence that we are dealing here with two different affixes is the fact that the nominals of *N#able* and *V#able* are formed by different rules. The denominal adjectives always take the nominal ending *#ness* and never *+ity* (*fashionableness, *fashionability; sizableness, *sizability*), while the deverbal adjectives show no real preference (*acceptability, acceptableness; moveableness, movability*). We can account for this difference most easily if we regard the two sets as separate and formed by different rules. Slightly less palpable evidence comes from the fact that the two *#ables* have very distinct semantics. The deverbal one means approximately 'capable of being Xed (where X is the base)'. The nominal one means 'characterized by X (where X is the base)'. This difference shows up in cases in which a form *X#able* can be derived from homophonous noun/verb pairs. If we are dealing with two affixes, then it is in only these instances that the word *X#able* should be ambiguous between the two senses noted above. Though there are few cases, the evidence is favorable. *Fashionable*, which may be either deverbal or denominal, has the two senses 'in fashion' and 'capable of being fashioned'. Similarly, *sizable* means 'of great size' and 'capable of being sized'. Such a consistent correlation of homophony and ambiguity can only be accounted for on the hypothesis that we are dealing here with two different affixes, each with its own meaning and each with its own base.

The unitary base hypothesis is a strong assumption and easily refuted. One must merely show that a certain WFR operates on two distinct classes of bases.[3]

[3] The word *distinct* is important. It is not sufficient to demonstrate that a suffix attaches to both nouns and adjectives, for example. There are ways to formalize these two as constituting a single class within the extended standard theory of Chomsky (1972a). However, if a WFR applied either to adjectives or to transitive verbs (two classes which could not be subsumed under one without including others as well), then we would have a counterexample. Similarly, the rule investigated must be a reasonably productive one, for, as we have seen, less productive rules tend to be less coherent, and we should naturally expect more variation and exceptional behavior with such rules.

4.1.2. The Output

The most studied aspects of morphology, at least the aspects most studied within the framework of generative grammar, are the relation between the syntax and semantics of the base and that of the output of a WFR, the common properties which the two share, and the ways in which these relations and commonalities can be accounted for. The scope of these matters is large and, if only for reasons of space, I will not take up the subject in this monograph. We will simply assume the existence of some mechanism for representing the relations in question, satisfying ourselves solely with the syntax and semantics of the output itself.[4]

Neither will we take up the question of "possible meaning"; whether, independently of morphology, there are formal and other constraints on the meanings of words. Much of the work on lexical decomposition, though it may seem to be related to morphology, is really addressed to this question.[5]

Syntactically, every new word must be a member of some major lexical category, the exact category being determined by the WFR which produces the word: #*ness* produces nouns (*redness*) and #*able* adjectives (*definable*). The output can assume the form of a labeled bracketing in which the syntactic category of both the base and the output are specified and the base is represented by a variable. So, for example, the WFR which attaches +*ee* (discussed briefly above) forms nouns from verbs. This is represented as follows:

(5) $[+[X]_V +ee]_N$

---

[4] In the literature on the syntactic relationships between the base and output of what I call WFRs, one sort of fact is usually overlooked: though it is often noted that many features are mapped from the base onto the output of the rule, it is seldom mentioned that there are some which are lost. In many cases the loss is idiosyncratic, but sometimes it is systematic. Consider the following example.

The two verbs *break* and *show* allow specific prepositional phrases (PPs) to follow them:
   (i)   They broke the glass *into six pieces*.
   (ii) We showed the film *to the children*.

To each of these verbs there corresponds an adjective of the form *X#able*: *breakable*, *showable*. These adjectives may not be followed by the corresponding PPs:
   (iii) *The glass is breakable into six pieces.
   (iv) *The film is showable to the children.

Without the PPs, the sentences are acceptable:
   (v)   The glass is breakable.
   (vi) The film is showable.

One cannot explain this distribution on the grounds that adjectives do not allow such PPs to follow them, since specifically those adjectives of the form *Xable* which are not regularly derived from verbs do allow such PPs:
   (vii) This object is visible to the naked eye.

Nor can we invoke semantics, since the passive construction, which some (e.g. Chapin (1967)) have claimed to be involved in the derivation of *X#able* forms and which roughly paraphrases the *X#able* form, also allows these PPs:
   (viii) This glass can be broken into six pieces.
   (xi) This film can be shown to children.

It would thus appear that an externally unmotivated feature of the WFR *X#able* forbids PPs which are subcategorized by the verb *X* to appear after the adjective *X#able*. What this means is that the simple view of a WFR as consisting of a purely additive function must be revised.

[5] Among the recent work in this area I can recommend Horn (1972). Of the traditional sources, Ullmann (1957) is the most comprehensive.

Semantically, the meaning of the output of a WFR will always be a function of the meaning of the base.[6] This function is the meaning of the WFR itself. Traditionally, the meaning of a WFR is represented by a paraphrase containing a variable. So, for example, the agentive occupational suffix #*er* can be roughly paraphrased as in (6):

(6) $V\#er_N$ 'one who Vs habitually, professionally, . . .'

This meaning is exemplified in words such as *baker*, *programmer*, and *diver*. Such paraphrases should not be taken to be theoretically significant. Hopefully, a well-developed theory of semantics will provide some better representation than mere paraphrase.

Paraphrase also misleads one into thinking that the peculiarities of a rule such as the one attaching #*er* are specific to it; that this is a rule of English and completely unrelated to any rule of any other language. This is not true. Many other completely unrelated languages have similar "one who Vs" nominals, and in these too modifiers such as "habitually, professionally" are also often valid. Modifiers such as these are also a puzzle for those who would wish to derive *V#er* from *V* by a simple syntactic-like operation. Words like *habitually* are not usually lost in the course of syntactic derivations, yet such must be the case if we wish to derive *baker* from *bake*. Traditional labels like "abstract nominal" are sometimes more helpful, and more able to account for the data, than paraphrases. Consider the two English affixes +*Ation* (as in *derivation*) and #*ness* (as in *porousness*). The first is a "deverbal abstract nominal" and has the meaning 'act of Xing, or act of being Xed'. The second is a "deadjectival abstract nominal" and has the meaning 'fact or state of being X, extent to which something is X, or quality of being X'. The sets of meanings as expressed in the paraphrase are mutually exclusive; there is no way for $X\#ness$ to mean 'act of Xing', nor can $Xation$ have any of the meanings of $X\#ness$. Intuitively, this is because the latter is deadjectival, and hence cannot denote an action, and the second is deverbal, and hence cannot denote a fact, quality, or degree. Intuitively, also, the paraphrases are not accidental. We know what a "deverbal abstract nominal" must mean, and what a "deadjectival abstract nominal" must mean. Yet a statement in terms of paraphrases makes it all accidental. We have no theory that tells us what the meaning of $X+Ation$ and $X\#ness$ must and must not be.

As expected, the same sorts of information that a WFR is sensitive to are the sorts of information it can introduce. Even such things as lexical presuppositions can be introduced by WFRs. Looking again at the suffix *re#* studied by Williams (1973), we find that this suffix, as well as demanding of its base that its meaning involve a change of state, has a separate presupposition of its own. Consider the following sentences:

(7) John washed the dishes.

(8) John rewashed the dishes.

The second sentence presupposes that the dishes were washed by someone (not necessarily John), at some time previous to the time of the action of the verb of that sentence. The presup-

---

[6] This statement must be qualified by the further condition that the meaning of the output is determined by the base, but the strength of this prediction is determined by productivity, which is correlated with the morphology of the base (cf. below and chapter 3).

position is similar to the one entailed by the adverb *again*. It is separate, however, from the presupposition on the base. This is indicated by the fact that though I may hit someone again (in accord with the presupposition of the output), I may not rehit him (since *hit* does not meet the condition on the base, as noted in 4.1.1). Though no other WFR has been studied so carefully as this one with respect to its semantics, I suspect that others may be just as complex in their regularities.

4.2. Morphology

4.2.1. Morphological Restrictions on the Base

4.2.1.1. Abstract Morphological Features. It has long been recognized that the vocabulary of English is divided, for purposes of morphology (and to some extent phonology), into two distinct parts, *native* and *latinate*, and that there are many rules which are sensitive to this distinction. There are probably even further subdivisions, into *greek*, *romance*, etc.

A well-known phonological rule which is restricted to *latinate* items is the rule of Velar Softening (SPE, 219-223), which palatalizes *k* and *s* only in latinate forms. There are in addition many WFRs which are restricted to *latinate* bases. A good example is the suffix +*ity* (*oddity* is the only exception I know of to the restriction); it contrasts very nicely in this regard with its rival #*ness*, which does not discriminate at all between *latinate* and *native* words. WFRs restricted to native words are less common. One is the suffix #*hood*, of *motherhood* and *brotherhood*.

The most important thing to be noted about a feature like *latinate* is that it is abstract, much like an abstract syntactic feature. A question then arises as to what this abstract feature is a property of, words or morphemes? There is good evidence that the feature *latinate* is a property of morphemes. If such a feature were a property of individual words, then we would expect that different words containing the same morpheme would behave differently with respect to rules sensitive to the feature in question. This is not so. All words containing the morpheme +*ity*, for example, are *latinate*. This can be shown by the fact that all words of the form *Xicity* (*lubricity*, *felicity*) undergo Velar Softening, which, as noted, only applies in *latinate* forms.

Further evidence that it is the morpheme which is at least the basic carrier of the feature *latinate*, and also good indication of the abstract and arbitrary nature of the feature, is the fact that monomorphemic words tend to move into the *native* classification. For example, #*hood*, though restricted to *native* bases, attaches to words which are etymologically *latinate*, as in *priesthood*, *statehood*. But it is only monomorphemic words which are "exceptional". This makes sense if we are dealing with a feature which is both a property of morphemes and arbitrary. We expect monomorphemic words to lose this feature easily.

Stronger evidence comes from words which are made up of both *native* and *latinate* morphemes. Remember that the suffix +*ity* attaches only to *latinate* forms. Among the classes of words to which it attaches most productively is that of deverbal adjectives of the form

X#able (*advisable, digestible*). This class includes words like *doable, readable,* and *knowable*, which have native bases. *+ity* attaches to these words. *Readability* and *knowability* are well-attested. With regard to the feature *latinate*, these words have the structure [−latinate] [+latinate] [+latinate]. Since it is really the affix *#able* which is triggering the attachment of *+ity* and this affix is *latinate*, we can still preserve the statement that *+ity* attaches to *latinate* items only, in its simplest form, if we say that *latinate* is not a property of words but rather of morphemes.

Finally, and most convincingly, we can only account for the phonology of this last class of words if we assume that the feature *latinate* is a property of morphemes and not of words. As we have seen, a word like *forgiveable* has the structure [−latinate] [+latinate]. Remember that the phonological rule of Velar Softening applies only in [+latinate] items. If we assume that, when it is attached, an affix like *#able* causes the entire new word to be [+latinate] (by some sort of feature percolation), then the *g* of *forgiveable* would be in the proper environment for Velar Softening, since *forgive* is now [+latinate] and should undergo that rule. This does not happen. Nor does it ever happen that a phonological rule "overapplies" in this manner. A morpheme like *forgive* never becomes [+latinate] for the purpose of phonology. This general fact can only be accounted for if we assume that abstract morphological features are properties of morphemes and not properties of words.

Thus, one sort of morphological condition on the base of a WFR is a condition on abstract morphological features like *latinate*. From the above examples at least, it is possible to assume that a WFR will only be sensitive to the morphological features of that morpheme which is adjacent to the point of attachment of the morpheme of the WFR. A suffix would thus only be sensitive to the morphology of the last morpheme of the base, as in the last case, where *+ity* was only sensitive to properties of *#able*. Similarly, a prefix would be sensitive only to properties of the first morpheme of the base. We could then rule out the possibility of a suffix's being sensitive to the first morpheme of the base and a prefix's being sensitive to the last, and build up a theory which dictated the impossibility of these cases. A morpheme-based theory, for example, in which words are just strings of morphemes, could very easily incorporate such a restriction, and in a natural manner. Within the theory we are constructing, according to which words are formed from words and the base of every WFR is a word, it would not be so simple to incorporate such a general condition, for at the point of attachment of an affix the whole word and its morphology are present, not just the adjacent morpheme. As we shall see, this simple assumption is false. There are suffixes which are sensitive to initial morphemes. This fact is in a very roundabout way evidence for our general theory, for though we might think on a priori grounds that a system in which conditions could only be stated on adjacent morphemes and never on noncontiguous morphemes is simpler, within our theory it is difficult to see how it could be.

WORD FORMATION RULES

4.2.1.2. Restrictions Statable on Individual Morphemes. More tangible restrictions than [+latinate] are common. Most of these are of a positive nature and are correlated with productivity. Thus +*ity* attaches most productively to bases of the form *Xic*, *Xal*, *Xid*, and *Xable* (Marchand (1969, 314)).

I will give two examples of positive conditions that cannot be stated on adjacent morphemes. The first is simple. The deverbal nominal suffix #*ment* attaches most productively to verbs of the form *en+Y* and *be+X* (*encroachment, bewilderment, embezzlement, bedazzlement*) (cf. Marchand (1969, 332)). As noted above, this single example refutes the simple theory just proposed as to the nature of morphological restrictions.

The second example is a more complex one. It involves the negative prefix *un*#, which, as Siegel (1971) has demonstrated, attaches only to adjectives. (Specifically, she shows that nouns of the form *un#X* are derived from adjectives.) This prefix attaches most productively to deverbal adjectives, a class which includes present and past participles (*unflagging, unburied*) and words in deverbal #*able* (*unbearable*). The first two types are difficult to analyze, since they involve inflectional categories and perhaps drift as well. However, the class of adjectives in #*able* is clearly identified by its last morpheme, and *un*# is a prefix.[7]

There are also negative restrictions, cases where a certain WFR does not operate on bases of a certain morphological class. A simple example of such a restriction is one on #*ness*. As noted above, this suffix is not restricted from attaching to [+latinate] bases. However, it does not attach to adjectives of the form *X+ate*, *X+ant*, or *X-ent*: *decent*, *decentness, *aberrant*, *aberrantness, *profligate*, *profligateness. There are exceptions, but they are not common: *accurateness*.

A more complex case of a negative restriction also involves internal constituent structure, but that matter is clearer here than in the above case of internal structure. The rule in question involves the denominal adjective suffix -*al* (*global, organizational, regional*). This does not attach to the class of nouns of the form $X_V ment$ (i.e. the class of nouns of the form *Xment*,

---

[7] One question which arises in connection with these three classes is whether they are indeed three, or actually one: the class of directly deverbal adjectives. The case is not clear. There are restrictions on each of the three separate subclasses: verbs with particles are treated differently for each. With past participles, the particle is generally tacked on:

   (i)   uncalled-for, uncared-for

With present participles it is always dropped:

   (ii)   uncaring, unthinking

With #*able* the particle is sometimes retained and sometimes dropped:

   (iii)   unreliable, ungetatable

When the particle is retained, the derivative has a "jocular tinge", as noted in Marchand (1969, 202). Also, prefixed forms are treated differently in each case. If we are dealing with one class, then we must be able to account for the differences in an interesting manner while still preserving the utility of the notion *single class*. If we are dealing with three classes, then these differences need not be explained at all.

where X is an independently occurring verb). The restriction is exemplified in the list below:[8]

(9)
ornament	*orna$_V$	ornamental
excrement	*excre$_V$	excremental
regiment	*regi$_V$	regimental
fragment	*frag$_V$	fragmental
employment	employ	*employmental
discernment	discern	*discernmental
containment	contain	*containmental
derangement	derange	*derangemental

The constraint in question depends on internal constituent structure and not merely on the existence of a related verb or on some possible derivation of *Xment* from a verb.

If we are constrained by sheer existence, then a problem arises with nouns of the form *Xment* from which verbs are derived (cf. chapter 6):

(10) He complimented me on my dress.

(11) Don't experiment with such things.

(12) Life is so regimented.

Since these verbs all correspond to nominals, and the derivation of *Xmental* is not blocked (*experimental*, *regimental*), the constraint cannot be stated merely in terms of existence, but rather must refer to internal constituent structure.

Nor, though it seems simpler, can we extend the argument to all *Xments* derived from (derivable from) verbs. Such words as *excrement*, *increment*, and *medicament* can be derived from the verbs *excrete*, *increase*, and *medicate* by a rule of obstruent deletion before #ment (obs → ϕ/ _ _#ment). But the result is a structure in which X is not strictly a verb, having lost

---

[8] There are two exceptions to our rule:

(i) government govern governmental
    development develop developmental

In terms of sheer number, these are trivial. Walker (1936) lists about 500 words of the form *Xment*, of which the great majority are X_V*ment*. Also, the semantics of one of the derivatives, *governmental*, is curious: the noun *government* has at least two distinct senses. One is directly deverbal, the other extended:

(ii) His government of the country has been roundly criticized.
(iii) His government was defeated by a wide margin.

The sense of *government* in (ii) is that of a deverbal abstract action noun, and is similar to that of most deverbal abstract nouns in such diverse suffixes as #*ment*, +*Ation*, #*al* (*curtailment*, *finalization*, *denial*). The sense of the same word in (iii) is an extended substantivization, similar to that of *organization* in (iv):

(iv) The organization needs you.

The exceptional adjective *governmental* has only one sense, corresponding to the extended sense of *government*, that of (iii):

(v) The funds were used for purely governmental purposes.

The difference between the two senses of *government* can be represented in purely structural terms as being that between *Xment* and X_V*ment*; *governmental* is clearly derived from the former. If, therefore, we state the constraint on X_V*ment*, then *governmental* is no longer an exception. Whether the same can be said of *development* I do not know, as its exact meaning is not clear to me.

This structural solution would also cover cases such as *departmental* where, though *depart* is an independently occurring verb, *department* is not derived from it.

its final consonant. This distinction is of course very fine, and it depends on the assumption that obstruent deletion is a real rule. If it does hold, however, it shows that we are dealing not with some sort of global constraint of the form "X is derived from Y", but rather with one on the structure of the base *at the point* of the application of the WFR. The case, if real, is interesting, because it makes a distinction between a global and a structural element, and it obeys the more restricted structural statement.

We must conclude that there is a constraint against the application of the rule *-al* to bases with the structure $X_V ment$. This restriction cannot be explained away on general syntactic grounds. Normally *-al* attaches quite freely to other deverbal abstract nominals: *organizational, observational, reverential, preferential*.

There is a negative restriction, similar to the one above in involving internal constituent structure, on *+ity* derivatives of words of the class *Xous*, a class discussed in detail in chapter 3. There are no *+ity* derivatives of adjectives of the form *Xferous* (the largest class of *Xous* adjectives). Thus there are no nouns of the form *Xferosity* (*coniferosity*, *herbiferosity*) and no nouns of the form *Xferity* (*coniferity*, *herbiferity*).[9]

4 2.2. Encoding Morphological Restrictions. How do we go about encoding these conditions within a theory of word formation? The most obvious method is to simply list them as conditions on the bases of WFRs. Thus, we might state a negative condition such as the one on *+al* as follows:

(13) $X]_N\text{-al}]_A$
    Condition: $X \neq [Y]_V ment$

Similarly for positive conditions, which, since they are correlated with productivity, will also assign some probability to the rule.

However, such direct statement is the limiting and least interesting case, and many seemingly independent conditions on WFRs can be attributed to other factors. Most negative conditions are the simple result of *blocking*, a phenomenon discussed in chapter 3. Blocking prevents the listing of synonyms in a single stem. An affix which is productive with a given morphological class will thus block the attachment of rival affixes to that class. At first glance, this blocking may look like an independent negative condition on the blocked affix. For example, we noted that *#ness* does not attach to bases of the form *Xate*, *Xant*, and *Xent*. This, however, is merely a result of the fact that the rival affix *+cy* does attach productively to these classes (and no others but *Xcrat*): *profligate/profligacy, decent/decency, aberrant/aberrancy*. The productivity of *+cy* thus blocks the application of *#ness* in these cases.

As we have noted, blocking is basically a constraint against listing synonyms in a given stem. In general, among rival rules only the rule which is most productive with a given class will be able to fill the slot for a given stem in that class. Of course, the productively formed item

---

[9] There may be semantic reasons for this, as none of the adjectives admit of degree modification, and it seems in general difficult to nominalize adjectives having this restriction. Thus, even *#ness* derivatives of *Xferous* are odd: ?*coniferousness*, ?*herbivorousness* Notable exceptions are *vociferousness* and *soporiferousness*, whose bases admit of degree.

may drift and in drifting leave its meaning slot, in which case another may take its place. The result is more than one item of a given class in a given stem, but not with the same meaning. Such is the case with *humanity* and *humanness*: the first has drifted. Similarly for *recital* and *recitation*.[10] Note that we are not excluding the possibility that two words will occur with the same meaning but rather that there should be two words with the same meaning and the same stem in the same person's lexicon at the same time. To exclude having two words with the same meaning is to exclude synonymy, and that is ill-advised. It is also quite possible for two different speakers to have two different words in the same stem with the same meaning and for one person to forget the word he has in a particular slot at a particular moment and to make up another one, for the moment. In fact, the blocking rule, stated as a condition on the filling of slots, predicts that the fewer the number of stably filled slots one has, the more likely one is to accept new words. This seems intuitively correct.

The blocking rule cannot account for all morphological restrictions. First, it can only account for negative ones, and it does not even account for all of these. The impossibility of the attachment of *-al* to $X_V ment$ cannot be traced to blocking, simply because there is no other form to block it. Therefore, some of the negative morphological restrictions on WFRs, and all of the positive ones, must be stated independently.[11] I will review the one proposal which has been made in the published literature for a method of encoding these restrictions, that of Chapin (1967, 1970), and then go on to propose an alternative and, I hope, superior method of dealing with them.

4 2.2.1. Ordering of WFRs. It has been proposed by Chapin (1967, 1970) that WFRs must be ordered in a similar manner to syntactic rules. This is impossible within our theory, for the ordering of WFRs requires that speakers always carry out derivational processes for complex words, and the improbability of this forms the basis of the present work. It is therefore imperative that we demonstrate on independent grounds that the ordering hypothesis is untenable in spite of its initial appeal.

Ordering is a well-known device in syntax and phonology. Chapin (1967) notes that if we have reason to believe that WFRs are syntactic rules, and if we have reason to believe that there can be extrinsic orderings placed on syntactic rules, then we have reason to suspect that there

---

[10] No nominal suffix seems to be productive with the class *Xcite*: *citation, incitement, excitement/excitation*. This does not mean, however, that we will have more than one noun in a given slot, merely that within the class of verbs of this form the affix chosen will not be predictable.

[11] One negative condition which can be accounted for by something other than blocking is the following: it is impossible to form verbs from comparative adjectives of the form $X_A er$. The only verbs formed from comparatives are *better* (formed by a very productive φ rule), *worsen*, and *lower*. Note that the first two are formed on irregular comparatives. Now, on the assumption that only words in the lexicon can be used as bases for a WFR, and on the further assumption that only irregular words can be listed in the lexicon, it will follow that since most #er comparatives are perfectly regular they cannot be listed in the lexicon and hence cannot serve as bases for any verb-forming rules. The reason for the occurrence of *better* and *worsen* is thus merely the exceptional quality of their bases: they are irregular, hence listed, and hence candidates for bases. The sole remaining exception is thus *lower*, and it is peculiar in several ways. First, the adjective *low* has no associated verb, though most of the other common adjectives in its semantic class do: *deepen, heighten, widen, lengthen*. The reason for this is that the affix *+en*, which we will discuss below, does not attach to words ending in vowels (*grayen*). The existence of *lower* can perhaps be attributed to this complex of factors.

may be extrinsic ordering relationships among WFRs.

Prima facie, there are good reasons to believe that WFRs are not syntactic rules. The fact that words persist, and all the concomitant properties of words which this fact gives rise to, is one. A second reason involves the function of WFRs, compared with that of other rules.

What do syntactic transformations do? Given a deep structure, we apply to it the ordered set of transformational rules and arrive at a surface structure. If we decide, for one reason or another, to stop somewhere in the middle, applying the first half of the rules and forgetting about the rest, there is no guarantee (in fact it is highly unlikely) that we will produce a recognizable surface structure. This is because the entire set of transformations is really one huge rule or algorithm for converting a deep structure into an equivalent surface structure. The same is true of the ordered set of phonological rules.

However, such is not the case with WFRs. As their form implies, the application of any one WFR, which is always a rule for forming a word from a word, will give us a word. There are no intermediate abstract stages. Nor do these rules take us from one level of the grammar to the next as syntactic and phonological rules do. They do not turn an X of one level into an equivalent X of another level. Rather, they add something to an X, something at once phonological and semantic, and produce a Y which is an element of the *same* linguistic level as X and is not at all equivalent to or corresponding to X. It is thus quite clear that WFRs and transformations do not *do* the same thing. Therefore it is highly unlikely that WFRs will be ordered among syntactic transformations.

This does not mean that WFRs cannot be ordered. It merely means that there is no special reason for expecting them to be ordered among themselves. The type of ordering that has been proposed to exist among WFRs, it should be noted, is *arbitrary extrinsic* ordering. An extrinsic ordering is one that is imposed on two rules which, a priori, could appear in one order or another. The extrinsic ordering tells us that of two rules A and B, A applies first. There are nonarbitrary extrinsic orderings; such orderings are determined by external principles like the cycle in syntax, or the finer principles of Williams (1974). An arbitrary ordering is one which is not governed by any general principle, but must be stated specially for a particular pair of rules. This type of ordering is of course the least desirable, since it is the least constrained. As a matter of fact, all suggested arbitrary ordering hypotheses in the linguistic literature have been slightly stronger than this minimal one. Arbitrary extrinsic orderings are transitive; that is, if A precedes B, and B precedes C, then A precedes C.

Let us look at an example of how arbitrary extrinsic ordering can be used to account for morphological restrictions on the base of a WFR. Consider the following contrast. The suffix #*ism* attaches productively to words ending in -*al*:

(14) *constitutional#ism*
physical#ism
animal#ism

However, -*al* does not attach to words ending in #*ism*:

(15) **dogmat ism al*
*fatal ism al

This restriction cannot be attributed to the syntactic class of the words ending in #*ism*, since -*al* attaches to other abstract nouns: *inspiration*$_N$*al*$_A$. Nor is the concatenation *Xismal* generally prohibited:

(16) *strabism al, dismal, catechism al, embolism al, rheumatism al, baptism al*

These last items crucially differ from those in (15), however, in that the *Xism* form is not derived by any rule; there exists no corresponding free form *X*:[12]

(17) *strab, *dism, *catech, *embol, *rheuma, *bapt

Ordering of the relevant WFRs can handle all this material quite nicely. Rule B, the #*ism* rule, whose output is essentially $[[X]_A \#ism]_N$, is extrinsically ordered after rule A, the -*al* rule, whose output is $[[X]_N al]_A$. This ordering guarantees the impossibility of words of the form $[[[X]_A \#ism]_N al]_A$, i.e. the words of the type we wish to exclude. It permits us to generate words of the type (14), since to generate these rule A must apply before rule B, which our ordering permits. It also allows us to generate the words in (16) (*strabismal*) since the #*ism* in these cases, in a theory of word-based word formation, is not attached by a rule. We see, then, that the ordering handles a relatively complex set of data in a simple manner.

There is a mechanism which will produce the same result as ordering, at least when one is dealing with constraints on concatenation. One can simply state the negative concatenation conditions. So, one could put a negative condition on the base of rule A, which would say that A, -*al* Attachment, never applies to words of the form $[X \#ism]_N$. This will have exactly the same effect as ordering the rule which attaches #*ism* after that which attaches -*al*. There are several differences between the two theories, all of which weigh in favor of ordering, if we consider the power of the two. First, negative conditions on the base can refer to nearly any property a base could have, whereas ordering restrictions, in terms of what they can actually restrict, are much less powerful. Since conditions can encode all that ordering encodes, and then some, we must prefer ordering until it is shown that we must have recourse to the extra power the other device provides us with. The second way in which the two differ is with regard to multiple conditions on one rule. If it is perfectly transitive, the ordering theory makes certain very strong predictions, which the other theory is incapable of handling. If, in addition to the two rules above, which had the property that the output of B could not serve as the input to A, we have another rule C, whose output cannot be the input to B, within the ordering hypothesis, this situation forces us to order C after B. But this ordering, by transitivity, predicts that C cannot ever precede A, and predicts, completely independently of anything but ordering, that the output of C cannot be the input of A. Within the condition hypothesis, on the other hand, the fact that the output of C cannot serve as the input to B is an isolated fact, encoded as a negative constraint on B, with no predicted side effect on A. Within this theory, there is no reason why the output of C cannot be the input to A. The ordering theory thus makes a prediction where the other is silent. We must therefore prefer the ordering theory, and we must look at its predictions to see whether they are always correct.

[12] We will disregard the possibility and associated complication of *baptism* being derived from *baptize* and *catechism* from *catechize*.

With regard to the last issue, i.e. that of transitivity, Chapin adduces several examples which force the rejection of a complete transitive ordering. I will repeat one only. *+Ation* attaches to verbs in *#ize* (*standardization*), *#ize* attaches to adjectives in *-al* (*industrialize*). *-al* attaches to nouns in *+Ation* (*organizational*). Within the ordering theory we then have an ordering of the following sort:

(18) a. *+Ation* precedes *-al* (*organizational*)
 b. *-al* precedes *#ize* (*industrialize*)
 c. *#ize* precedes *+Ation* (*organization*)

If the ordering of WFRs is completely transitive and linear, then this is impossible, as *+Ation* both precedes and follows *-al*. Within an ordering hypothesis, we must have recourse to some sort of cyclic ordering here if our ordering claim is to have any force at all. As Chapin (1970) notes, because WFRs are all optional, the simple cycle of syntax is equivalent in their case to no ordering at all. If we place all WFRs in a cycle, then any WFR may follow any other WFR immediately, given enough cycles. This leads Chapin to propose what he terms an *epicycle*, whereby all WFRs are placed in a linear order by extrinsic conditions, and rules which apply cyclically, as in (18), must be adjacent to each other in the complete linear order. Thus *+Ation*, *-al*, and *#ize* will be immediately adjacent to each other, in the order given, and these three may be epicycled on. Possible epicycles will be marked off by some device. (See Chapin (1970) for a more detailed discussion of the epicycle.)

As Chapin stresses, the epicycle is a highly suspect construct. It does have the virtue of being refutable. A possible counterexample, which Chapin rejects on grounds which I have discussed in another context (cf. 4.2.1.2), is *governmental*, whose derivation violates an epicycle (cf. Chapin (1970, 62)).

A more likely counterexample is the class of words of the form *Xatorial* (*dedicatorial*, *investigatorial*). Chapin establishes the order *al–ize–ation*. He shows that within an epicyclic theory the order *ation–al–ize* is incorrect. We mentioned in chapter 2 that Martin (1972) had established that words of the form *Xory* are derived from words of the form *Xion*. This fact establishes an extension of the ordering to *al·ize–ation–ory*. However, the class of words *Xatorial* shows that *-al* must follow *ory*. This ordering is a violation of the epicycle. Words of the form *Xatorial* thus refute the ordering theory even in its weakened epicyclic form, and we are led back to the less desirable alternative of simply stating conditions.

With regard to the first issue (that is, what sorts of things can be conditions on WFRs), there is more substantial evidence that the ordering theory is incorrect. First of all, WFRs must refer to abstract features like *latinate*. As noted above, the *+ity* rule must refer to this feature since it only attaches to *latinate* words. However, since many of the words to which *+ity* can attach are not derived, it must be possible to state the specification for *latinate* bases independently of ordering, i.e. as a condition on the base of the *+ity* rule. Thus there is need for such conditions even within a theory involving ordering.

WFRs must also occasionally refer to the stress pattern of the base. Siegel (1974) discusses two such cases, both of which will be described in detail below. Stress is generated by phonological rules, and, as Chapin makes clear, it is impossible for a theory of conditions on WFRs which attempts to incorporate all these conditions into ordering statements to deal with such phonological conditions. Since there is no reason to doubt the reality of the phonological conditions which Siegel discusses, and there is no way to encode them into any other sort of restrictions, we must admit that they are strong evidence against the ordering theory.

Another major problem which the ordering theory faces is that of coexisting forms. To see how this is a problem, we must first review Chapin's account of the distribution of the nominal affixes #*ment* and +*Ation*. Citing an unpublished work by Emonds (1966), Chapin states that the distribution of these affixes is by and large governed by phonological properties of the base: verbs with the prefixes *eN-* and *be-* take #*ment*; verbs ending in oral or nasal stops take +*Ation*; verbs ending in *v* or *z*, preceded by an optional liquid, nasal, or peripheral stop, preceded by a lax vowel, take +*Ation* (*starve, sense, fix*); verbs ending in a liquid preceded by a vowel take +*Ation* (*console, explore*). All others take #*ment*. We can account for these data by ordering +*Ation* before #*ment* and marking verbs in *eN-* and *be-* as exceptions to +*Ation*. There are of course many exceptions, which are noted, but "the generalizations are striking." In addition, all other nominal affix rules are ordered before these two (*-al, -ence*, etc.). This serves to eliminate the application of either of these rules to stems which have nominals occurring with the other affixes (*occur/occurrence/*occurment/*occuration*).

We will not consider the empirical validity of Emonds's constraints. Rather, we must ask exactly what ordering is being used to encode here. It seems quite clear that ordering, when used with rival affixes, is being used to encode the blocking constraint. The reason we do not find **occurment* or **occuration* is because we already have *occurrence*. The same is true at least of the fact that +*Ation* does not attach to stems beginning in *eN-* and *be-*. First and most important, using ordering to encode the blocking facts obscures the actual function of the blocking. It predicts that there will never be pairs of nominals in the same stem, which is false. It is perfectly possible to have more than one nominal in a given stem, as long as the nominals do not have the same meaning. This fact is exemplified in the list below:

(19) *ment/ation*
 consolement consolation
 assignment assignation
 al/ment
 committal commitment
 ence/ment
 condolence condolement
 ϕ/ment
 advance advancement
 escape escapement
 abandon abandonment
 al/ation
 approval approbation

recital	recitation
proposal	proposition
ure/ation	
striature	striation
juncture	junction

Another problem, of course, is the establishment of disjunctive environments. Even Emonds runs into this problem. Because words which begin in *eN-* and *be-* may otherwise meet the conditions for +*Ation* attachment, all the words which begin in these prefixes must be made exceptions to the +*Ation* rule by some sort of rule feature marking device. Though it is possible to preserve the ordering theory by having recourse to such a device, the fact that one must have such recourse merely serves to show that ordering is being overextended in these cases and should be reexamined. We must conclude that ordering should not be used as a device to encode blocking, first because it predicts blocking where there is none, and second because the ordering can be established only by an abuse of the notion "disjunction".

I have not mentioned the fact that ordering is a most unsatisfactory device for encoding positive conditions on the base of a WFR. The fact that #*ment* attaches to verbs which begin in *eN-* or *be-* can be noted only derivatively. If a WFR is not ordered before the rule whose output is a certain form, then certainly this rule can apply to the output of that rule; but there is no way for ordering to express the fact that there is a certain affinity between WFRs and certain bases, that is, that a WFR will be more productive with certain bases than with others. As long as #*ment* attachment is ordered after the *eN-* and *be-* prefix rules, it may operate on verbs having these prefixes, but there is no way to encode the fact that it *prefers* these.

For all of the above reasons, ordering cannot be used as a device for encoding restrictions on the morphology of the base of a WFR. I have dwelt on the question of ordering for three reasons. First, arbitrary transitive linear ordering is a relatively highly constrained device for dealing with certain morphological conditions on the base of WFRs, and as such deserves consideration. It is also the only device for dealing with such phenomena which has been proposed in the literature. Second, it has been proposed, though we may question the logic of the proposal, that since we know other sorts of rules (specifically syntactic rules) to be ordered, then if we discover WFRs to be ordered in the same manner we have some justification for believing that WFRs and syntactic rules are related. We have shown that ordering is not a good device for dealing with conditions on the base of WFRs. We therefore have no reason to suspect that WFRs are ordered among themselves. This is a very strong indication that WFRs are not in the same class as syntactic rules but form a separate, self-contained set of rules. This gives added weight to the proposal that word formation is accounted for by a component of the grammar which is distinct from all others. Last, ordering of WFRs is impossible within the general framework of this monograph.

4.2.2.2. Unordered WFRs. We must conclude from the above section that WFRs are not extrinsically ordered among themselves. The only possible ordering among WFRs will then be intrinsic, which means in effect that WFRs are unordered. Within such a system, the morphological conditions on the base of each WFR must simply be stated for each rule.

Most negative restrictions will be accounted for by the blocking rule and thus will never have to be stated independently. Therefore, the fact that *-al* does not attach to bases of the form [X] #ism]$_N$, which we dwelt on at length above, need never be stated directly, because words of this form are usually subject to the rival rule of *-ic* (*modernism, modernistic*) (cf. chapter 6 for justification of this derivation).

Positive restrictions, which can never be encoded into an ordering framework, are different. They are closely correlated with productivity, and productivity is a variable matter. Rules cannot simply be classified as productive or not productive; rather, there are degrees of productivity. It is therefore interesting that we can associate this variable property of productivity with the morphological composition of the base of a WFR, for it is just this one property which is not unique: a WFR operates on bases of different morphological classes.

Apart from the few cases in which a WFR has no morphological conditions on its base,[13] the productivity of a WFR will always be associated with the individual morphological subclasses of the base, rather than the unitary syntactic base of the rule. Thus, the productivity of *+ity* will not be a function of the whole class of *latinate* adjectives, but rather of each of the morphological classes *Xile, Xous, X+able*, etc. It is these classes which comprise the morphological conditions on the base, conditions which must be stated independently for each WFR and separately from the syntactic, semantic, and phonological operations of the WFR itself.

Now, as we saw in chapter 3, semantic coherence varies with productivity. Since productivity is associated with morphological conditions, then semantic coherence must also be so associated. This removes semantic coherence and productivity from the main body of the WFR to the conditions on it. The semantics, syntax, and phonology of the main part of the WFR will be purely discrete. The form, meaning, and category of the output will be a compositional function of the base. This allows us to preserve such statements as "#*ness* forms deadjectival abstract nominals." A completely discrete relation between the base and the output will, however, be true only of the ideal and most productive cases. The less productive a rule is with a given morphological subclass of its base, the less coherent the semantics.

Note again the importance for such a system of the unitary syntactic base hypothesis (4.1.1). If we did not have a unitary syntactic base for every WFR, there would be no way to isolate any discrete operation. The unitary base hypothesis can be tested empirically, and independently of any other of the claims I am making. Our theory thus depends crucially on several different hypotheses, each of them independently falsifiable, yet whose consequences are completely interrelated.

Summing up so far, we can say that a WFR has at least two parts. First, there is a part which specifies the syntactic and semantic characteristics. There will be no disjunction in the specification of these characteristics, and no negation. The semantics of the output of the WFR

---

[13] Such a one is deverbal #*able*, which, though it has no morphological conditions on its base, is intuitively felt to be very productive (cf. Chapin (1967)). Note that not all WFRs without morphological conditions on them are necessarily productive. The rule of *+ous* (*bilious, contagious*), which has no morphological restrictions on it to my knowledge, is decidedly nonproductive.

is specified here as a compositional function of the base. Second, there is a series of positive conditions on the morphology of the base. These conditions are associated with productivity and semantic coherence (which are, in a sense, the same thing).

I will give a simple example, the rule of negative $un\#$. I will assume for the moment that the phonological part of the change of the rule consists of the addition of the prefix and its boundary: $un\#$.

(20) *Rule of negative $un\#$*
 a. $[X]_{Adj} \rightarrow [un\#[X]_{Adj}]_{Adj}$
    semantics (roughly) $un\#X$ = not X
 b. Forms of the base
    1. X_V en (where *en* is the marker for past participle)
    2. X_V #ing
    3. X_V #able
    4. X+y (worthy)
    5. X+ly (seemly)
    6. X#ful (mindful)
    7. X-al (conditional)
    8. X#like (warlike)

(Of course, each of these will have some index of productivity and coherence associated with it. The list is given roughly in order of productivity. Remember that the mere fact than an item is not in one of the listed classes does not preclude it from undergoing the rule, unless it is subject to a negative condition.)

4.3. Phonology

4.3.1. The Phonological Operation

I have said that a WFR specifies a base, as well as some operation on the base which results in a new word. This operation will usually have some phonological reflex, some morpheme which is added to the base. We will call this operation the *phonological operation* of the WFR.

The operation is generally quite simple, and consists of the addition of some affix to the base. The WFR specifies the phonological form of the affix and its place in relation to the base. The rule of #*ness*, for example, adds [ness] to the end of the base. We will assume that the affix and its position are constant for a given WFR. This means that #*ness*, at least when introduced by the rule of #*ness*, is always a suffix and always has the form #*ness*. Nor does this rule give any other form which it might add instead of #*ness*, in some particular environment. The affix is a phonological constant. We will also assume that the boundary associated with the affix is a constant. This means that if we find two affixes which are phonologically identical except for the boundaries associated with them, they cannot be introduced by the same WFR.

We assume that the phonological form is constant and completely specified. No archiforms or abstract segments are allowed, in accord with the theory of Kiparsky (1973). We will see in chapter 5 that the phonological form of an affix, though it must be fully specified, may have different realizations in environments determined by the morphology of the base. These different forms, called *allomorphs*, are introduced by a later set of rules called rules of *allomorphy* (cf. 5.3). It is significant that these allomorphs are determined not by individual bases, but by the morphemes of the bases, and by morphemes in the most extreme sense of the term: semantically empty roots. This is parallel to the fact that productivity is determined by morphological features of the base. It is also susceptible to parallel treatment; it can be removed entirely from the main body of the rule. All morphologically determined variation thus lies outside the WFR itself. Furthermore, variation can be totally ascribed to morphological properties of the base.

4.3.1.1. Copying Rules. The general phenomenon of reduplicated or copied affixes controverts the simple statement that affixes have a phonologically constant form. Reduplication rules copy one part of the base of a rule and use this part as an affix or part of an affix. They are clearly morphological rules of word formation. First, there is no reduplication rule whose environment is totally phonological. (We are of course referring only to total copying rules, not to rules such as harmony rules which assimilate features of one segment onto another.) Second, reduplication rules are never ordered among the rules of the phonology. Both of these statements are easily falsifiable, but if they are true, they are sufficient to demonstrate that reduplication is not a phonological process. Reduplication rules are often said to have a "function" which is the same as that of WFRs. The notion is a little obscure, but we will take it to be correct and will assert that all copying rules (*not* assimilation rules) are WFRs. However, it is clear that if they are WFRs, then the affixes introduced by them cannot be called phonologically constant.

Consider for example the well-known Klamath vowel copy rule (Kisseberth (1972)). There are prefixes in Klamath which have fixed consonants, but whose vowels are copied from the initial vowel of the stem:

(21) a. *Noncausative* *Causative*
pe:wa 'bathes' hespe:wa
no:ga 'is cooked' hosno:ga
ma:s?a 'is sick' hasma:s?a

b. *Noncausative* *Causative*
qe:gi 'is absent' sneqe:gi 'loses something'
qdo.ča 'rains' snoqdo:ča
tsa:ktgi 'become light (in weight)' snatsa:ktgi

c. *Nonreflexive* *Reflexive*
ne:sla 'has sexual intercourse from behind' sene:sla
lo:čwa 'covets' solo:čwa
twa:qa 'smears' satwa:qa

The three prefixes all have different vowels in each case, the vowel being the same as the first vowel of the stem. Kisseberth gives evidence that the vowel of the prefix, though it must be present in underlying phonological representation, cannot be shown to be represented in this underlying form by any one of the surface vowels of Klamath. He therefore has recourse to an abstract segment V*. The prefixes are listed in their underlying forms as hV^*+, snV^*+, and sV^*+. A phonological vowel copy rule applies only to V*, and replaces it by the first vowel of the stem in all instances. Within the theory being put forth here, and the theory of Kiparsky (1973), V* is not a permissible underlying segment and the rule of vowel copy is an impermissible rule of absolute neutralization. However, it is only by using an abstract segment like V* that we can preserve the hypothesis that the morphological operation of a WFR produces a phonological constant. It seems to be impossible to preserve both hypotheses; either we give up the prohibition on abstract segments, or we give up the phonological constant. This dilemma will be forced upon us in all instances of copying rules.

However, the dilemma can be easily resolved. We have hypothesized that all copying rules are WFRs and that they are never ordered among the rules of the phonology. Kisseberth specifically notes that both of these are true of the Klamath vowel copy rule: both that it may be considered "morphological", and that "It is significant that no phonological rule must precede Vowel Copy, to my knowledge" (Kisseberth (1972, fn. 7)). This is fine, if we are only worried about the abstractness of phonological representations and are willing to allow abstract segments which are concretized by morphological rules prior to the phonology. But we are trying to make the even more restrictive claim that morphemes cannot be represented with abstract forms. The simplest way to retain this claim is to revise somewhat the view of a morpheme as a phonological constant. We will therefore view a morpheme not as a constant but as an operation.

Though morphemes are usually regarded as entities with independent status, just like stems, this is not the only possible way of looking at them. It is equally possible, and perhaps preferable, to regard a morpheme as a product of a phonological operation associated with a WFR. In the case of a phonologically constant affix, like #ness, there is no difference between the two treatments. However, when dealing with copying rules, if we wish to preserve the statement that no morphemes contain abstract segments at any level of derivation, we come to a quick decision between the two views of the morpheme. We simply replace the notion of a morpheme as a phonologically constant entity with one of a morpheme as the product of a unique phonological operation. This simple claim allows us to replace the Klamath causative prefix hV^*s with the following rule:

(22) *Klamath Causative WFR*

$$_V[C_0 \ V \ X]$$
$$1 \quad 2 \quad 3 \ \rightarrow \ _V[h \ 2 \ s \ _V[1 \ 2 \ 3]]$$
$$\text{Caus} \quad -\text{lg}$$

This rule will produce correctly all the forms of (21a). Similar rules will give us all the other forms of (21) and can be used for all other copying affixes. We no longer need worry about abstract morphemes since by stating the copying rule and the rule which spells out the morpheme in the same rule we have avoided the intermediate point in the derivation at which the abstract segment occurs. This will always be possible if we are right in claiming that all copying rules can be ordered before phonological rules, for this claim implies that no rule will come between the rule which attaches the morpheme and the rule which spells out the copied segment(s) of the morpheme.

By accounting for copying by rules like (22), we are making three claims:

(a) Copying operations are parts of WFRs and are not phonological rules (the latter claim is already implicit in Kiparsky (1973)).
(b) WFRs are not labeled frames. (Rules like (22) cannot be represented by labeled frames.)
(c) Affixes, unlike stems, have no independent existence.

A possible objection to the encoding of copying operations into rules like (22) is that the use of such a device entails that if we have n affixes which contain copied material, we have n copying rules. If every affix contains a copied vowel, the "same" vowel, as in the case of the three Klamath rules discussed so far, then we must repeat the same operation for each affix, in this case three times. It seems intuitively incorrect to have to do this. The objection, it should be noted, is not one of substance, but rather one of manner: it is not that the incorporation of copying rules into WFRs prevents us from handling the data, but rather that it forces us to handle a certain array of data in an inelegant manner.

The theory which uses abstract segments, however, faces much more serious problems: there are types of copying rules which it is intrinsically incapable of describing. For example, in Klamath there is another reduplication prefix, which copies the first C_0V of the stem (the V is short as above). Note that this prefix copies not just the first consonant, but the entire first consonant cluster. This is exemplified in the following paradigm:

(23) *Nondistributive*   *Distributive*
     pe:wa 'bathes'   pepe:wa
     no:ga 'is cooked'   noṅo:ga
     ntopa 'spoils'   ntontpa
     qniẏa 'has an erection'   qniqnẏa

Since the number of consonants in the affix is equal to the number of consonants in the stem, and since this number varies with the stem, there is no way in which we can represent the consonants of this stem by abstract segments. This is so because sometimes the stem will contain one abstract segment, and sometimes two, and how many it contains is predicted by the stem. The vowel of course can be represented as V*. What Kisseberth does is to invoke a "morpheme of reduplication" which he calls R. R is realized by a rule as a copy of the initial consonant (cluster) of the stem plus V*. This rule is called Reduplication, and it is followed by Vowel Copy. This is a very awkward solution, for it uses a copying rule of the form of (22), as well as an abstract segment; in fact, the copying rule *introduces* the abstract segment. Abstract segments are bad enough; when such segments are introduced by rules, and exactly the sort of rules which, as far as I can see, the abstract segments were designed to avoid, the system becomes very suspicious indeed. The above example demonstrates clearly the need for copying rules of the form and function of (22) in any system, and it shows that such copying rules are the source of abstract segments. This fact is bad for the theory which, by using abstract segments, allows us to state vowel copy as one rule, for it casts doubt on the validity of the abstract segments.

The general phenomenon of syllable copying is immensely troublesome for the abstract segment system. Consider the Hebrew *Pilpe:l* conjugation, which is formed by reduplicating monosyllabic roots:

(24) Root   *Pilpe:l*
      kul   kilke:l 'sustain'
      gal   gilge:l 'roll'

We will not discuss the vowel pattern, which is characteristic of all active stems of the form CVCCVC. For the moment we can assume that the vowel of the root is copied and that a later rule adjusts the vowels. Within the system proposed, in which rules of the form (22) are permitted freely, and in which there are no abstract segments, the derivation of *Pilpe:l* forms is simple. If we use abstract segments, on the other hand, the matter becomes immensely complicated. If we represent the reduplicated part (we will assume the first syllable is the copy) by C*V*C*, then we do not know which stem consonant is copied onto which C* unless we have two copying rules: one for the first consonant, and one for the second:

(25) a. *Initial Consonant Copy*
        $C \rightarrow C_j / \#\_\_\_VC+C_jY\#$
   b. *Other Consonant Copy*
        $C \rightarrow C_j / X\_\_\_CVC_j\#$

Assuming another rule for copying the vowel, we have a total of three copying rules for this one affix. Furthermore, they are rules that cannot be generalized to any other segments, for they will only apply to those *Pilpe:l* forms. None of these rules can even be extended to the one other conjugation which is formed by copying. This is the much more common *Piře:l* conjugation, which is formed by doubling the middle consonant of the triliteral root as follows:

(26) root   *Qal*   *Piře:l*
      gdl   ga:dal 'grow'   gidde:l 'raise'
      šbr   ša:bar 'break' šibbe:r 'smash'

If we disregard the problem of the infix, which will be treated below, the system allowing abstract segments requires the following rule for the reduplicated middle consonant.

(27) *Middle Consonant Copy*
      $C \rightarrow C_j / [_{\text{root}} CVC_j\_\_$

The root marker is there to ensure that the rule does not apply in the *Hiřil* form. One could alternatively restrict the rule to C*. In any case, whatever the exact formulation of this rule, it is not the same as either of the rules of (25). We need three consonant copy rules for two affixes, none of which has any other justification, all of which apply to abstract segments only, and all of which can be ordered before any other rule of the phonology (there is no ordering among them).

All of these idiosyncrasies arise from the desire to state the Klamath copy rule once only, instead of three times. This desire leads us to posit four rules (including vowel copy in *Pilpe:l*) of no generality at all. This last example demonstrates perfectly the fallacy behind the rule counting argument. One theory gives us more rules in one case (Klamath) and the other theory gives us more rules in the other case (Hebrew).

Do we decide between theories idiosyncratically for each language, depending on the number of rules each theory needs? It seems wiser to disregard rule counting, and to ask what other sorts of things the two theories are saying. If we ask this question, it is clear that the theory which regards copying rules as a particularly complex sort of WFR is preferable. This theory predicts that copying rules will always apply at a certain point in the derivation of words, namely before the phonology, and hence that they will never follow any rule of the phonology; it rids us in a principled manner of a class of abstract segments which are problematic and undesirable on general grounds; it says that all copying rules are "functional", i.e. WFRs; and it gives us more clues as to the general form of WFRs. All of the claims of this theory can easily be falsified, and they are many. The other theory, which treats reduplicated segments as abstract phonological entities, makes no interesting and restrictive claims at all as far as I can see.

Note that I have not disproved the abstract segment theory. It is probably not very easily disproved, if at all. What I have done is to indicate that the advantage which this theory seems to enjoy over the one I am proposing is illusory at best, and not very interesting in the general case.[14]

Summing up this section on copying rules, I have claimed that all copying rules are WFRs, and that the phonological operation of a WFR, rather than spelling out a completely specified phonologically constant form, is in itself a unique phonological operation. If both of these claims are true, and we will assume them to be so, then we cannot state WFRs as simple labeled frames; rather, we must state them as transformations. This in turn helps us to differentiate formally between the affix and the stem, items which intuitively are very different. Another point of this section is the fact that if we treat copying rules in a certain way, i.e. as WFRs, then we can ban such rules from the phonology. This result is the first phonological conclusion of this monograph, and I think that, if correct, it is a very important one. What I have done so far is to elaborate a theory of derivational morphology on grounds which are completely independent of phonology (except, of course, that I have accepted a particular theory of the phonological component, well-motivated on phonological grounds, that of SPE, and on certain finer points, that of Kiparsky (1973)). Despite the fact that my theory of morphology is not built

---

[14] For those who like to anticipate, it should be noted that copying rules cannot be allomorphy rules, simply because they are completely independent of the morphology of their base. No matter what the morphology of the base, the copying rule is always the same. If we found different copies in different morphological types of stems, then we might want to use a rule of allomorphy.

on any phonological grounds, it has proven useful in solving a phonological puzzle of great particularity, that of abstract copied segments. It is the possibility of this sort of interaction which led me to investigate the entire area of morphology, in the hope that by discovering what was legitimately morphological we might be able to determine what legitimately belongs in other components of the grammar as well. We see here the first case of the (hopeful) success of this general method.

4.3.1.2. Infixing. We have asserted that copying rules are WFRs, mainly on the grounds of "functional" similarity. We have been able to assert further that WFRs cannot be written as simple labeled frames, because copying rules cannot be so written. However, because of the tenuous nature of the logic here, it would be better if we had independent grounds for the latter assertion. Such an independent reason is the impossibility of describing infixes in terms of labeled frames. Consider as a simple example the matter of the Hebrew *Pi̇r̩e:l* form, which is produced by reduplicating the second consonant of the root. The reduplication problem, which we have discussed, is independent of the question of where the copied consonant goes. As we see from the examples of (26), the copy goes next to the consonant it is copied from, and the rule has the effect of doubling the second consonant of the root. How can such a rule be stated? How do we specify the position of the copy? The copy goes *inside* the root, and therefore we must be able to factor the root, in order to know what inside position the copy takes. Such a factorization is impossible if we restrict the statement of WFRs to labeled frames.

For the sake of clarity, and in order to avoid the problem of copying that arises in this example, let us look at a very productive English infixing rule. The English infix *fuckin*, first studied to my knowledge by Siegel (1971) and which more or less has the function of expressing a certain attitude on the part of the speaker, occurs in words like the following (from Siegel):

(28) Monòngà–fúckin–héla
Sànta–fúckin–Crúz
fàn–fúckin–tástic

The infix is restricted to stems which have a 3-1 stress pattern. Furthermore, it can occur only immediately before the 1 stress, as the following unacceptable forms show:

(29) *Monòng–fuckin–ahéla
*Túr–fuckin–in
*Chì–fuckin–cágo
*Chìcko–fuckin–pèe

Siegel states the rule for infixing *fuckin* as follows (1971, 10):

(30) *Fuckin Rule*
$$[X \overset{3}{V} C_0 (\begin{bmatrix} V \\ -str \end{bmatrix} C_0)_0 \text{ [infix] } \overset{1}{V} Y]$$

The trouble with using such a labeled frame to express the rule in question is that there is no place in the rule where the base is specified as an independently existing entity. The rule as stated has no way of expressing the notion "formed from". It is incapable of encoding this notion and that of "infix" in a single string, because the infix is inserted inside the base (this is after all the meaning of the term *infix*). In order to be able to express these two notions, we must be able to factor the base string and insert the infix between two of its factors, as shown below:

(31) *Fuckin Rule (revised)*

$$[X \overset{3}{V} Q \overset{1}{V} Y]$$
$$1 \; 2 \; 3 \; 4 \; 5 \rightarrow 1 \underset{3}{,} 2 \; 3 \text{ fuckin } 4 \; 5$$
where Q contains no $\overset{1}{V}$

This statement of the rule allows us to express both the idea "formed from" and the infix. The form of the rule is the same as that of copying rules like (22). All infixing rules must have this form. The general phenomenon of infixation thus provides very strong evidence, independent of copying rules, for the impossibility of using labeled frames to express the phonological operations of all WFRs. This is assuming that the rule which places the infix in its proper position is a WFR and not a rule of the phonology, i.e. that it is not ordered among the rules of the phonology. This assumption will be discussed in a later section and is, as far as I can tell, essentially correct.

4.3.1.3. Consequences. We have found two classes of rules which are best viewed as WFRs, and which force us to state WFRs in a particular manner, namely as transformations. This is different from the system using labeled frames mainly in that it forces us to divide the rule into two parts, a structural description and a structural change. The first part specifies only the base. The second part contains the base and the result of the operation of the WFR, amalgamated into one unit. The formal nature of this bifurcation has an intuitive counterpart: the base is an independent entity, which we know already, for in order to qualify as a base it must be an independently occurring word and a member of a major lexical category: the affix (which in most cases is equivalent to the affixing operation) cannot be separated from the rule, because it is nowhere given any representation of its own. This intuitive counterpart is very different from the view which people normally have of affixes: namely, that they are independently existing entities; that they are morphemes, just like stems, and have all the properties stems have.

This view has led to many problems, of which I will mention only the two most commonly discussed. The first problem is that of discontinuous morphemes, like the Semitic vowel patterns. Though I cannot claim to have solved all the mysteries of Semitic morphology, it is clear that once we stop thinking of these vowel patterns as items of the same sort as the stems, we can stop worrying about the metaphysical import of these discontinuous patterns and begin to develop a framework within which they can be studied. Another problem which this view of WFRs relegates to the status of an artifact is that of the *zero morpheme*. In English, there are WFRs with which no morphophonological operation at all is associated. Though the base undergoes semantic and syntactic changes, sometimes of a complex nature, nothing happens to its form. The most productive of these WFRs forms verbs from nouns. The semantics is very complex, and I do not know exactly how many rules are actually involved, but I have listed a few examples of different types below:

(32) | Noun | Verb |
|---|---|
| father | father |
| referee | referee |
| butter | butter |
| cement | cement |
| spear | spear |
| club | club |
| ship | ship |
| skate | skate |
| nail | nail |
| hammer | hammer |
| bale | bale |

Within a theory in which WFRs are represented by labeled frames (or even simple concatenations, as the simplest theory supposes), how do we represent rules like the above? The answer is the zero morpheme. The rule taking *father* to *father* can be represented as follows:

(33) $[[\text{father}]_N \phi]_V$

We can then refer to this ϕ as the suffix for forming verbs from nouns. But the concept of a formless phonological substance like this is abhorrent, even ridiculous when we realize that for every WFR which has no associated phonological operation (and there are several in English (cf. Marchand (1969, 359-389))), we must posit a separate such entity, with a resulting proliferation of zeros, one for every rule: $0_1, 0_2, \ldots, 0_n$. Though the zero morpheme is not a necessary entity in a theory which uses labeled bracketings to represent WFRs (the theory of SPE uses labeled brackets and no zero morpheme), it is quite clear that in the theory being put forth here the zero morpheme has no place at all.

Last, we should note that the problem of a morpheme as a meaningful entity, discussed at length in chapter 2, though not resolved within the framework being put forth, can now be reduced to the problem of whether a WFR has meaning, since a morpheme is not independent from the WFR which introduces it. The problem of the meaning of a WFR has been approached by dividing a WFR into two parts: the central part, all of whose operations and elements are unique, compositional, and discrete (the base; the phonological operation; the semantic interpretation of the output as a function of the semantics of the base; the syntax of the output); and the morphological conditions on the base, which determine productivity and the semantic coherence of the individual output. Within such a framework, what should be constant about the "meaning" of an affix is the syntactic category it is a marker of, since the syntactic category of the output cannot vary with productivity. This constancy is true to a very great extent. Words drift, and monomorphemes, as noted in chapter 2, can drift just about anywhere, but morphologically complex words do not drift out of their syntactic categories. Also, rules which have no phonological reflexes, like the rules involved in the derivation of the items in (32), generally do not apply to morphologically complex bases. There is a miniscule number of exceptions to this observation, among which are *proposition*$_V$, *referee*$_V$, *waitress*$_V$, *dirty*$_V$, and *muddy*$_V$. Marchand's explanation of this restriction is the fact that "suffixes are categorizers". The fact that suffixes are such strong markers of category is what we are predicting.

An interesting result of this last fact is that we can now have a somewhat finer view of the use of WFRs as rules of morphological analysis. When we encounter a word we have never heard before, one thing we can know pretty much for certain is the syntactic category of the word (if it is polymorphemic); and this is about all we can know for certain, since this is the only constant part of the WFR, the only part which is unaffected by the morphology of the base. Once we isolate the affix and the syntactic category of the putative base, we can look at the morphology of the base; if we know the meaning of the base, we can make guesses as to the "distance" of the newly encountered word from the base, on the basis of the coherence of the rule, which we know from the particular morphological category of the base. If the base is not a word, we know, as noted, nothing but the syntactic category of the new word. If the base is not a word, but is a member of a morphological category which is productive, we know more about the new word. If I have never heard the word *tangible* before, I know that it is an adjective, and that is all. On the other hand, if I hear the word *solemnization*, though I may not know the word *solemnize*, I know that the WFR of *ation* is very productive with bases of the form *Xize* and hence know that I am dealing here not merely with a noun, but with an abstract deverbal action. I think this conclusion is correct, though quite obviously it must be subjected to experimental verification.

4.3.2. The Place of the Phonological Operation in the Grammar

WFRs have been viewed as rules for adding new words to a dictionary and rules for analyzing existing words. They are once-only rules; a word is made up by applying a WFR, and the newly made up word is added to the dictionary. The phonological operation has been claimed to be simultaneous with the other parts of the rule, and to be separate from the rules of the phonology. No part of a WFR can be a phonological rule, orderable among the rules of the phonology. Rather the word is formed entire, as a completely phonological entity, prior to all the rules of the phonology.

But this cannot be true. Consider the *fuckin* rule discussed above. The infix must be inserted in a word which has a 3 – 1 stress contour, and it must immediately precede the 1 stress ($\overset{3}{K\bar{a}lama}$ $\overset{1}{fuckin-zoo}$). In order to know exactly where to insert the infix *fuckin*, we must know the stress contour of the base. But the stress is determined by relatively regular phonological rules. Therefore, the infixation process must be ordered after some phonological rules. The only way in which we can enter *Kalamafuckinzoo* in the dictionary entire, and not with some abstract marker, like [fuckin infixation], is to give up the entire theory of phonology and enter the word in its surface form. This is something we do not want to do.

It appears that rules of infixation and copying are different from other WFRs, in that their morphological operations (which, as we have seen, depend crucially on the actual base) can be ordered among the rules of the phonology. The question that we must now ask is how they are ordered among the phonological rules. If they are just phonological rules like any other, a possibility which we have repeatedly denied on external grounds, then they will have the same ordering properties in a phonological derivation; they will be subject to such phenomena as reordering. If, however, we can show that these rules will intervene in the phonology only at a specific number of places, then they are not phonological rules in the common sense.

To see how a rule could intervene in the phonology without being orderable as a rule of phonology, we must review the general conception of the structure of the phonological component as outlined in SPE. In that work, phonological rules are sharply bifurcated into cyclic and word-level rules. Exactly what sorts of rules are cyclic, and what sort are word-level, is a problem not discussed in SPE, and I have nothing to say on this matter. Cyclic rules apply first, cyclically, the limits of each application being determined by bracketings, which, we have argued, are determined by the morphology. Word-level rules are postcyclic or last cyclic, and apply only once. From this outline, we see that there are several points at which a rule might intervene in the phonology, without being ordered strictly between two phonological rules. The rule might apply before the cyclic rules, as we have argued most morphological operations do; it might be ordered between two cycles; it might be ordered after all cycles, but before word-level rules; or it might be ordered after all word-level rules, that is, after the phonology. If we allow a phonetic component to follow the phonology, then these latter rules could conceivably follow morphological operations.

I think that it is possible to restrict the application of the phonological operation of a WFR to three places in the phonology: first, before the phonology, as has always been assumed; second, before the word-level rules; third, after the phonology. Such a restriction on the place of these operations allows us to retain the position that WFRs do not interact with phonological rules, though they may interact with the phonology. It puts us on a middle ground, theoretically, between the most restrictive structuralist phonemic views on the ordering of morphologically and phonologically motivated rules (morphemic precedes morphophonemic precedes phonemic) and the unrestricting views of Anderson (1975), wherein there is no necessary connection between type and order.

4.3.2.1. Reduplication Paradoxes. I will now present a discussion of selected reduplication processes in a variety of languages and show that the phonological peculiarities of these processes can be easily accounted for if these processes operate at the places designated above, and at no other places. The widespread peculiarities of reduplicated forms cannot be dealt with in any other principled manner.

The data for the following section come from Wilbur (1973). Transcriptions vary with her sources. Wilbur begins from the observation that reduplicated forms are often exceptional, at least when viewed from the theoretical standpoint of standard generative phonology. Their exceptionality lies in the fact that the reduplicated affix (R_r), and the part of the stem of which it is a copy (R_o), are often identical in their surface phonological representations. If we assume that reduplication is a morphological process which precedes all phonological processes, then this surface identity can sometimes only be attained at great cost, because the phonological rules, applying blindly, will produce different reflexes of R_o and R_r. The problem is to ensure that this will not happen, that R_o and R_r will be identical.

It is important to notice that this problem does not always arise. It is not always the case that the two are identical. The following derivation of an Akan[15] reduplicated form, from Wilbur, demonstrates how such a situation can arise:

(34) /dumʔ/ +Redup ($C_1 V_1 C_2$)
 Reduplication dum dumʔ
 Regressive Homorganic Nasal Assimilation dun dumʔ
 Progressive Nasal Assimilation dun numʔ
 Closed Syllable Vowel Nasalization dũn nũmʔ
 Output dũnnũmʔ

This situation is normal within a theory which assumes that all copying takes place prior to the phonology. The rules, which are independently motivated, apply in their proper order with no regard for extrinsic facts, i.e. that this is a reduplicated form; an incidental result of their application is that R_r and R_o are made dissimilar. This is the situation with which I am familiar. It holds in all the Semitic languages; in Greek, where the reduplicated initial consonant of the perfect prefix is subject to deaspiration; and, I am told, in Sanskrit. In all these familiar cases, if reduplication is prephonological, then everything goes through normally.

A simple example of an exceptional case is the following Madurese[16] form:

(35) kun 'order'   kunkun 'orders'

The form is exceptional because an otherwise general rule of nasal assimilation which would give us the form *kungkun has not applied. Nor is this an isolated form. Nasal assimilation does not apply to any reduplicated forms:

(36) bangbang   'wings'   *bambang
     b–ar–ing–bing 'stand on end'   *barimbing
     d–al–ang–dang 'tall and thin' *dalandang
     t–ar–əm–təm   'peaceful'   *tarəntəm

If the reduplication process precedes all the rules of phonology, then reduplicated forms must all be marked as exceptions to the phonological rule of nasal assimilation, for this rule fails to apply though its structural description is met. Wilbur presents several other examples of this sort of exception, where, within a conventional theory, we must say that a rule has failed to apply in a reduplicated form, with the result that R_o and R_r are identical.

All of these cases can be handled simply by ordering reduplication after the relevant phonological rule, in fact after all phonological rules. This device accounts for the nonoperation of the phonological rule and for the identity of the forms R_o and R_r. It is also possible to

---

[15] The Akan data and rules are from Schachter and Fromkin (1968).

[16] The Madurese data are from Stevens (1968).

achieve the same result by the proper manipulation of boundaries. Boundaries, however, will not suffice for the next class of phenomena.

A more curious type of exception, curious, that is, within the conventional framework, is one in which a rule seems to overapply; that is, it applies to a segment whose environment does not meet its structural description. In the following Chumash data, a rule of aspiration is involved which combines a voiceless consonant with a following h or identical consonant, to produce an aspirate.

(37) /k+kuti/ +Redup 'to look'

k+kut kuti	Reduplication
k^hutkuti	Aspiration

/ma+k+hawa?/ +Redup 'aunt'

ma+k+hawhawa?	Reduplication
mak^{h}awhawa?	Aspiration

We see that in these cases reduplication and infixation precede the phonological rule of Aspiration, which then makes R_o and R_r dissimilar. In the light of the examples in (37), consider those in (38):

(38)
Base	/s–soyin/	/ma–k–hatinet/
Redup ($C_1 V_1 C_2$)	s–soy soyin	ma–k–-hat hatinet
Expected	*s^{h}oysoyin	*mak^{h}athatinet
Actual	s^{h}oys^{h}oyin	mak^{h}atk^{h}atinet
Gloss	'it is very black'	'my joints'

The forms of (38) can be derived simply by ordering reduplication in these cases after Aspiration, in fact after all phonological rules.[17] The difference between the forms of (37) and those of (38) is due to the relation between the reduplication rule and the phonology in the two cases. In (37) reduplication precedes the phonology, in (38) it follows. Note that there is no question of Reduplication's being ordered among the phonological rules themselves. This is impossible, because the rule of Reduplication is not a phonological rule. I think the difference between the two sets of data gives striking confirmation to our theory, for it is just these two sets, and only these two sets, which our theory permits, and it is only these two which actually occur. Thus, by making one simple addition to the theory of morphology, we can account for all and only the observed irregularities of reduplicated forms.

There are other ways to account for the forms of (38). One could reduplicate the prefix as well as the first consonant of the root in these cases:

(39) s–soy–s–soyin   ma--k--hat–k–hatinet

Aspiration would then apply to produce the correct forms. But in this solution we have two very different reduplication processes, one of which produces the forms of (37) and the other

---

[17] A mechanism is required which permits reduplication of a surface segment s^h which is the reflex of two underlying segments $s+h$, only one of which is part of the root proper. Syllabic structure seems to be at work here, a matter which is not easily incorporated into the theory of phonology we are using. We will assume a convention which matches syllable boundaries with root boundaries on the surface. This means that a root begins with a consonant on the surface, if it can.

the forms of (38), whereas in the ordering solution the rule is the same and only its place is different. Since the utility of ordering has already been shown, and since the solution of changing the form of the rules does not have as general an application, we must suspect the latter in the same way we suspect a solution involving boundaries in cases like (36). Boundaries can handle cases like (36), and a change in the rule can handle cases like (38), but the ordering theory can handle both, and in a principled and highly restricted manner that cannot be claimed for the other solutions.

Munro and Benson (1973) discuss a complex set of data in Luiseño. Here reduplication interacts with a number of phonological rules, and the type of ordering which we have proposed provides a satisfactory analysis. I will only give a rough outline of the phenomenon, and the reader is encouraged to look at the original presentation.

Three rules are of import here. First, a rule of syncope deletes a vowel preceded by a short stressed vowel and a single consonant and followed by a single consonant and a single vowel:

(40) čáqʷi- 'to seize'   čáqʷla- 'to wrestle'

The second rule raises unstressed mid vowels to high vowels:

(41) hédi- 'to open'   hidíki- 'to uncover'

The third rule, which we will call SH, changes $č$ to $š$ before a noncontinuant or #:

(42) té:ŋališ 'medicine'   té:ŋaličum 'medicines'
      qé:ŋiš 'squirrel'   qé:ŋičum 'squirrels'

SH applies to the output of syncope:

(43) ʔé:či 'above'   ʔeškawis 'upper lip'
      móči- 'to weave'   móšlat 'belt'

Stress is governed by a complex set of rules, and it in turn governs certain vowel deletion and shortening rules that are discussed in the sources.

What is important for our purposes is the interaction of the above three rules with reduplication processes. Normally, Reduplication applies to underlying forms:

(44) *Sample Derivations*

	/čapomkat/	/čikʷi:-/
Redup C_1V_1	čačapomkat+um	
Redup $C_1V_1C_2$		čikʷčikʷi:-
Various rules	čačapomkat+un	čikʷičikʷi:-
Syncope	čačpomkat+um	čikʷíčkʷi:-
SH	čašpomkat+um 'liars'	čikʷíškʷi:- 'to suffer'

There is a class of reduplicated forms, produced by what is termed Adjective Reduplication, which always have the surface form $C_1V_1C_2V_2 - C_1C_2V_2 - š$:

(45) ʔáva- 'to be red'   ʔaváʔvaš 'pink'
      máha- 'to stop'   mahámhaš 'slow'
      sá:wa 'to wheeze'   sawáswaš 'hoarse'

This is the only reduplicated form which is deintensificative; it means 'a little' and not 'a lot'. These forms can be generated in the usual manner, with one exception. When the first consonant of the C_1C_2 sequence is a č, it does not undergo the SH rule as expected. Instead of *čarǎsrǎš, which is the expected form, we find čarǎčraš 'torn'. Similarly, we find čukáčkaš 'limping' and not *čukǎskaš. Note that if we do reduplication postphonologically we rid ourselves of the exception. We will write the rule as an infixing reduplication rule:

(46) *Adjective Reduplication Rule*
C V C V X#
1 2 3 4 5 → 1 2 3 4 1 3 4 5

The change in stress can be accounted for by including the infix $C_1C_2V_2$ in a class which is motivated independently and which attracts stress to the syllable immediately preceding it.

However, there are two problems which face this simple rule (46). First, by reduplicating $C_1C_2V_2$, instead of $C_1V_1C_2V_2$, a step which is necessary if we are to account for the fact that SH does not apply to these forms, we lose the possibility of accounting for the absence of V_1 by the perfectly well motivated and otherwise general rule of syncope. For, if we allow syncope to apply here, then how can we refuse to permit SH, which follows syncope (cf. (43)), unless we adopt the kind of exception marker we have been trying to avoid? There is no way to account for both facts in a principled manner within the ordering theory: the fact that SH has not applied, which is patent, and the fact that syncope could have applied. The second problem is the application of raising of *o* to *u* in čukáčkaš, from the stem čoka- 'to limp'. Since stress is not determined until after reduplication, it must be presumed that raising has taken place after reduplication, which is a problem if reduplication is postphonological.

The first problem I have no solution for. It is true that the vowel in question could have been deleted by syncope; it is equally true that our theory denies this and replaces what could have been analyzed as one process by two separate and unrelated ones. Note that there is no evidence that syncope must have applied. This brings us back to the problem of real generalization which we dwelt on without any conclusion when we first encountered reduplication rules. I have nothing further to say on that point.

The second problem is less trying. Raising is a late phonetic rule. Reduplication will apply before such rules, and hence raising will apply to its output. We can conclude that the Luiseño data, though they can be accommodated in our theory, cannot be completely explained by it. Whether this is a problem must remain unknown until we have a better idea of what we are trying to explain.

There is a conceivable type of "exception" which cannot be handled by ordering of any sort, and hence is beyond the power of our restricted ordering theory. Wilbur describes what such an exception would be: if a rule of the phonology, whose structural description is not met until after a reduplication rule has applied, and which applies to R_r (the reduplicated part), also applies to the corresponding segment of R_o, even though this segment is not in the proper environment for the application of the rule.

She gives a hypothetical example. Let us presume that a language has an intervocalic voicing rule. In this language, a form *inuk* could be reduplicated and then undergo the voicing rule, giving *inuginuk*, or it could be reduplicated after the voicing rule had a chance to apply and have the surface form *inukinuk*. Within any sort of ordering theory, there is no way to derive the third possible form, *inuginug*, in which the rule of voicing applies both to intervocalic *k* and to the final one, which is its "mate" in a certain sense of the term. Wilbur discusses at some length the sort of theory that could accommodate such a fact, and needless to say, it is much more powerful than the one I am proposing. Since the ordering theory, any ordering theory, cannot account for such an example, and Wilbur's can, we are left with an empirical issue and a question: Do such forms as the one exemplified by our hypothetical case ever appear in natural languages? If they do, then any ordering theory is incapable of dealing with natural language and must be abandoned. What we must do is go out and hunt for real cases.

Wilbur cites two "possible examples", both of which are isolated words. One is noted by her source as the only case of its kind in the language, and Wilbur quite correctly hesitates to say that it is crucial. The other example may be the result of a typographical error, for the author's discussion of the word in question seems to imply that it has another form (cf. Hill (1969, 362)).

The fact that Wilbur has been able to find only these two words, one of which is a unique exception in the language and the other of which may be spurious, seems to me to provide very strong evidence in favor of an ordering theory. Such a theory precludes words of this sort from being derived by regular morphological and phonological rules in a principled manner. Isolated forms whose derivation is uncertain cannot be considered as decisive evidence, except insofar as they are isolated.

4.3.2.2. Deletions. "Morphological" deletion rules are not common. Nor are they popular. In fact, such classic examples as Bloomfield's (1933) analysis of French adjectives have been reworked in such a way as to avoid the necessity of positing a deletion morpheme (cf. Schane (1968)). This unpopularity is understandable: within a framework in which a morpheme must have a constant phonological shape, deletion is even less substantial than ϕ; and, unlike reduplication, it does not lend itself to the straitjacket of abstract segments. Within our own framework, however, there is nothing abhorrent about a deletion rule, so long as it can be stated as a unitary phonological operation (as indeed the French rule can be). Now, if we allow reduplication rules to operate postcyclically, we should expect the same of deletion. In the case of deletion, the necessity of such an ordering will be transparent; the deleted entity conditions a phonological rule prior to its demise. Several examples of this type are discussed in Anderson (1975).

The clearest case is that of the Danish imperative, which is formed by deleting a final ə from the infinitive (if the infinitive ends in ə). Orthographically, the imperative is thus rendered identical to the stem. Phonetically, however, such is not always the case: the imperative often has a long vowel or consonant, or a *stød* (transcribed by ʔ), where the stem does not:

(47)   [bað] 'bath'   [spel] 'game'
       [bæːðə] 'to bathe' [spellə] 'to play'
       [bæʔð] 'bathe!'   [spelʔ] 'play!'

Anderson notes that there is a general phonological rule in Danish whereby a short vowel (or, in certain circumstances, the following consonant) is lengthened before a single consonant *followed by a vocalic ending*. Lengthening then determines the insertion of *stød*. Lengthening and *stød* insertion also take place in the imperative, where there is no vocalic ending. The simplest solution to this problem is to order the imperative rule (deletion of ə from the infinitive) after the phonological rules of lengthening and *stød* insertion. Within our framework, imperative formation is a WFR with a postcyclic or postphonological operation.

I will merely outline an analogous case in Abkhaz which Anderson presents. Here an agreement marking verbal prefix *y* is lost if immediately preceded by the NP with which it agrees. This rule (which is clearly syntactic) interacts with a very regular phonological rule of epenthesis which has the following basic form:

(48) $\phi \rightarrow ə / C\_\_CC \{ {V \atop \#} \}$

Examples: [yərtot'] 'they give it to him'
[yrərtot'] 'they give it to them'

y-loss, restricted to this one morpheme, and not applicable to other prefixes of the shape [y], must follow (48). This is evidenced by the fact that [yərtot'], in the proper environment, appears as [értot'] and not *[rtot']. Again a morphological (in this case syntactically so) rule follows the phonology. Note that in neither of the above examples is it the case that the morphological operation falls between two phonological rules. This is remarkable and in accordance with our theory.

4.3.2.3. Boundaries and Phonological Conditions. Siegel (1974) provides extensive evidence for the position that morphological operations apply at the level of the word as well as prephonologically. Siegel's theory divides English affixes into two classes: Class I, which is prephonological, and Class II, which is word-level. Evidence for her proposal comes from two sources: boundaries and phonological conditions on the base.

Boundaries first. Siegel associates the morpheme boundary + with Class I affixes and the word boundary # with Class II affixes. That Class II affixes should be attached after the application of cyclic phonological rules is almost self-evident: the sole purpose of this boundary in SPE (and its equivalent in Bloch and Trager (1942)) is to prevent the application of certain phonological rules, most notably stress rules (word-boundary affixes do not cause stress shift and are never stressed). The ordering which Siegel proposes immediately accounts for all the peculiarities of word-boundary affixes. Boundaries encode the place in the phonological derivation of the base at which the operation of a particular WFR takes place: + is prephonological, # is postcyclic (word-level), and we may assume that ## is postphonological.

The evidence from phonological conditions is more interesting. Traditional sources have remarked that WFRs are sensitive to phonological properties of their bases. As Siegel (1971) notes, the deadjectival verb-forming suffix *-en* is found attached to words which end in dental consonants, by and large. In fact, Marchand (1969, 272) notes that in the last 200 years only adjectives ending in *t* and *d* have served as bases for this rule. Exceptions to the rule date from an earlier, more liberal, period (*toughen, freshen, weaken*). The point of the example is to demonstrate that there are phonological conditions on the base of a WFR. Now, phonological representations differ from morphological representations in that a given morphological word has many phonological representations associated with it. There is the underlying representation, the surface, and all points in between. Whether WFRs can have access to any one of these levels is an empirical issue. What Siegel sets out to show is that the level at which the phonological conditions on the base of a given WFR are stated is the level at which the affix is attached, and only that level. This is a highly restricted and symmetrical system.

Now, since Class II affixes are postcyclic, they have access to information introduced by cyclic rules, most obviously stress rules. If Siegel is correct, we should expect to find stress-sensitive Class II (# boundary, unstressable) affixes, and no stress-sensitive Class I (+ boundary, stressable) affixes. This is the case.

The best-known example of a stress-sensitive affix is the nominal suffix #*al*. Ross (1972) noted that this suffix occurs only after a stressed vowel. The exact position for its attachment, as formulated by Siegel (1974), is after a stressed vowel followed by an optional sonorant followed by an optional anterior consonant:

(49) trial, denial, refusal, rehearsal, arrival, *constructal, *organizal, *resistal

The only exception to this rule is *burial*. That #*al* is a Class II suffix is clear from its not having any effect on the stress pattern of its base.

A similar example is #*ful*, which we have already discussed briefly in another context, and which is discussed at length by Siegel (1974), after Brown (1958).

We noted in passing that the infix *fuckin* was sensitive to the stress of its base. It is obvious that this phonological condition cannot be stated until the stress of the base is determined. In this case, however, it seems that we are dealing with a postphonological ## boundary infix. Both the base and *fuckin* have the stress contours that they would normally have in isolation, and the infixing affects neither one, at least in terms of their segmental phonology and the relative stress levels in the base and in *fuckin* considered separately. The 1-stress of *fuckin*, however, is subordinated to the 1-stress of the base, as shown below:

(50) Kằlamazȍo   fửckin   Kằlamafửckinzȍo

The ## boundary will automatically account for the subordination, since the Nuclear Stress Rule will apply as it does in compounds like *Madison Avenue*, giving the correct stress contour.

All of these affixes show a striking correlation among three things: the point at which the phonological condition on a WFR is stated, which is at least postcyclic, the point at which the operation of the WFR is performed, and the boundary associated with the affix.

4.3.2.4. Implications. We have seen the ramifications of a theory in which morphological operations can take place at certain very specific places in a phonological derivation. There is no question of these operations ever interacting with individual phonological rules.[18] We first

---

[18] A book might be more appropriate than a footnote here. There is a wealth of data from Tagalog and related languages bearing directly on the question of the ordering of reduplication and infixation rules with respect to phonological rules. Work has already been done by Carrier (1975) and Cena (1975) on these problems (within the general framework of this book). The fantastic complexity of the morphology of these languages, however, demands that deep and thorough study precede any statement from which important conclusions might be drawn.

showed that reduplication rules may operate at breaks in the phonology. The same was demonstrated for deletion rules and infixation rules. We then saw that this odd ordering is not due to the nature of these rules, which, unlike the more familiar varieties, must have access to the internal workings of stem and base in order to spell out the exact form and place of the affix they attach; rather, the same orderings apply for rules with constant affixes. The only difference is that because of the nonconstant nature of reduplicated and other base-dependent affixes it is easier to discern their interaction with the phonology than in simpler cases, where we must have recourse to evidence of a much more roundabout nature.

Our theory accounts for the peculiarities of the different morphological boundaries; boundaries encode the place in the phonological derivation of the base of a WFR at which the operation of the WFR is performed. Phonological conditions are also correlated with the operation: if an operation takes place at a certain point, then the phonological condition must be stated at that same point. There will therefore be as many different boundaries, and types of phonological conditions, as there are levels at which the operations of WFRs may take place.

There is still an important difference, however, between reduplication and other base-dependent rules and rules with constant affixes. In the case of the latter, boundaries serve a sort of global function: they encode the place of the phonological operation. We never need to repeat the operation, once we have formed the word, because the boundary will make sure that the affix is not processed by the phonology until the correct point in the derivation. With base-dependent rules, however, though the boundary must still be inserted (as we saw in the case of *fuckin*), the character of the role makes it impossible to use the boundary as a global marker. In cases where such rules apply at points other than the input to the phonology, there is no way to list the output of the operation in a lexicon without drastically altering our view of the nature of phonological representation and the role of phonological rules in a grammar. The WFR must carry an abstract marker like [+*redup*] attached to the base. At the appropriate place in the phonological derivation of the word, this marker triggers reduplication, infixation, or deletion. Such cases obviously contradict the general statement that WFRs are once-only rules, for word level reduplication and infixation cannot be so defined. I have not explored the further implications of this fact.[19]

4.3.3. Boundaries and Cycles

We are now in a position to correct somewhat the theory of the cycle first put forth in chapter 2. The basic claim made there was that the phonological cycle is determined by the morphology: there is a cycle for every affix which is the result of a well-formed WFR (which contains a word). This is not true. # boundary affixes block the application of cyclic rules. We have seen why this should be the case: such affixes are added at a point in the phonological derivation after the application of all cyclic rules. It follows from this that no cyclic rule will ever apply to them, that is, that they will block the cycle.

---

[19] We have already seen that the output of the most productive of WFRs must not be listed in the lexicon. These most productive rules are therefore not once-only rules either. We will see later (in chapter 6) that the type of phonological boundary usually associated with productive WFRs corresponds to the word-level and postphonological reduplication rules under discussion here. Hence, it is possible that there is an intrinsic connection between listing and phonology.

The following are then the basic claims of our theory insofar as it affects boundaries and cycles:

(A) There are as many types of boundaries as there are points in a phonological derivation at which WFRs may operate.
(B) The boundary is determined by the point of the operation.
(C) The phonological cycle is determined by + boundary WFRs: there is a cycle for every such WFR.
(D) There are no global phonological conditions on WFRs.

I do not think there is anything startling in the above theory. It tells us about the interaction of the morphology and the phonology. The morphology does not completely determine the phonology, as one might naively think, for every WFR must carry a boundary, and the cycle is limited to one type of boundary. Now we see the point of the assertion that every WFR has a constant boundary associated with it.

4.3.4. Problems

4.3.4.1. A Condition on the Surface Form of the Output. Aside from its other peculiarities, the deverbal affix #*ment* attaches productively to bases ending in the palatal stridents š, tš, dž (*abridgement, estrangement, impeachment*). This fact is correlated with the lack of productivity of the rival suffix +*Ation* with the same phonologically determined class. There is a curious reason for the nonproductivity of +*Ation* in these exact cases. The reason is that a rule of English phonotactics rules out the occurrence of two coronal fricatives in adjacent syllables. It is not only words in +*Ation* which obey this rule; the rule of #*ish* gives evidence for it as well:

(51) sheepish, piggish, *fishish, *drudgish

We are therefore dealing with a phonological surface condition which is completely independent of any one WFR. We can clearly see that the condition has reference to no other level from forms like *admonition*, as we shall see in chapter 5, this word is derived by the +*Ation* rule and not by a separate *ion* rule from *admonish* (which ends in the forbidden palatal strident), and it is permitted because it does not violate the condition *on the surface*.

Note that there is no question of globality. There is no constraint on +*Ation*, but rather a completely independent one which just happens to affect some otherwise possible +*Ation* forms. This is important: we have insisted that there are no global phonological constraints on WFRs and that all seemingly global phenomena must be traceable to other sources. This one is.

Returning to #*ment*, we can trace its productivity with bases in coronal fricatives to the completely external phonotactic rule. Because the +*Ation* forms are forbidden, no blocking applies here. The nominal slots of the verbs in question are open, and #*ment* fills them.

4.3.4.2. A Global Phonological Condition. There appears to be a rule-particular condition on the surface form of the output of the -*en* affix discussed above. In addition to the already noted condition on its base (ending in *t* or *d*), Siegel (1971) notes that on the surface -*en* must be preceded by one and only one obstruent, preceded by an optional sonorant, preceded by a vowel (*glisten, harden, dampen, whiten, frighten*). (I know of only one exception to this remark: *brisken*.) This restriction cannot be stated on the underlying form of the base, for there are forms like *fasten* and *soften*, with underlying obstruent clusters, which do not reach the surface because of the application to them of a rule which deletes *t* after an obstruent and before *n*. Furthermore, the condition cannot be a surface one, since there are words like *Boston* which violate it. *Boston* is not a problem for the *t* deletion rule, which can be written in such a way as to generate it and others like it properly. However, it creates a problem for our restriction, which must now become either a global condition on the *-en* WFR, or an accident.

If we can find one other rule besides *t* deletion which serves the function of converting the output of the *-en* rule from a form which is not in accord with the canonical pattern into one which is. then we have evidence that the canonical form is less likely to be an accident, and that we are indeed dealing with a global constraint on *-en*, which allows us to generate a word in this suffix just in case the word reaches the surface in the correct form.

The rule which meets this description is somewhat controversial, for it concerns a segment which undergoes absolute neutralization: the one written *gh*, presumed to be a velar fricative. Arguments for the existence of this segment as an underlying phoneme of English are given in SPE (233-234) and Pope (1972). The rule in question deletes *gh* before *t* in words such as *lighten, frighten,* and *straighten*. Believing in the rule presupposes our believing in the possibility of absolute neutralization, but if we do, then this is evidence that there is a global phonological constraint at work in the derivation of words in the suffix *-en*.

4.3.4.3. A Transderivational Constraint. A remark of Pope's, and of Siegel's, which the latter attributes to Morris Halle, suggests that a device even more powerful than the last is at work in the derivation of *-en* words. *-en* normally attaches only to monosyllabic adjectives, but there are several exceptions to this pervasive restriction. Pope notes that "*-en* attaches to the noun, rather than to the adjective, only when the adjective form would be unacceptable" (1972, 126). As instances of this she cites the words *heighten, lengthen,* and *strengthen. -en*, she claims, is attached to the nouns *height, length,* and *strength*, because they meet the pattern which *-en* demands, while the corresponding adjectives *high, long,* and *strong*, if concatenated with *-en*, would result in the forms **highen, *longen,* and **strongen*, which are unacceptable because of the surface constraint.

Pope's remark, however, is not correct. There are instances of *X-en* where *X* is clearly a noun with no morphologically related adjective. They are *threaten, hearten,* and *frighten*. In addition there is *hasten*, which might be derived from *hasty*, but which is more likely to be derived from *haste*. *Frighten* may be semantically related to *afraid*, but the morphological relation is only tenuous. It thus appears that of the seven denominal exceptions to the *-en* rule, three and a half can be explained by Pope's remark, while three and a half cannot. Additional evidence is hard to come by. The only adjective/noun pairs which meet the necessary requirements (that is, where the noun but not the adjective meets all the conditions) are those in which the noun is in *th* and the adjective ends either in a sonorant or vowel, or in an obstruent which is deleted in the course of a phonological derivation, i.e. *gh* or *ng*. The only pairs which meet this complex of criteria are *true/truth* and *slow/sloth* (the latter only if we are willing to stretch our tolerance). There are only two other monosyllabic adjectives in *ng* besides *long* and *strong*, namely *wrong* and *young*, of which one has no *th* nominal, and the other may be related to *youth*, though not by any rule of English. There are no other monosyllables in *gh* besides *high*.

Failing the possibility of any further evidence being procured, it would seem to be advisable, in this case at least, to reject the sort of device which an explanation like Pope's entails, despite the initial appeal of the explanation itself.

I would like to note in passing that in any case we are not dealing here with a phenomenon which is productive in any sense of the word. All the noun-based *-en* words are relics, dating from a time when the suffix was not so strictly adjective-based (except *frighten*, which is later). I have decided to separate word formation from word analysis just because of the fact that we run into such relics in morphology, as a result of the persistence of words. The case in hand proves the utility of such a separation, for it appears to be only in the analysis of relic forms that we must have recourse to the most powerful sorts of devices.

4.3.4.4. A Boundary Paradox. In one sense, this problem is illusory, and in another quite mysterious. On the simplest version of our theory, since + boundary affixes attach to underlying forms, and # boundary affixes to postcyclic forms, all the former should precede the latter. One should never find a + outside a #, for that would be paradoxical. Yet one does:

(52) a. b.
    analyze#able   analyze#abil+ity
    standard#ize   standard#ize+ation
    govern#ment   govern#ment+al

The paradox disappears when we remember that most WFRs are still once-only rules, and that the boundaries are relics of this one application of a WFR, which encode its effect in the phonology. When it was added, the #*ize* of *standardize* was added at the postcyclic stage in the derivation of *standard*. However, *standardize* now has an underlying form: /standard#i:z/. The only postphonological WFRs whose outputs cannot be entered as underlying forms are the infixation and reduplication rules. Now, since *standardize* has a legitimate underlying form, we can perfectly well add +*Ation* to it. The same goes for the other cases. As long as we regard word formation as a historical process, which is not repeated in every derivation, there is no problem. The problem only arises if we try to reduce the boundary-WFR pair, in which the boundary is a marker left for posterity by the WFR, to a simple WFR, which then must apply in phonological derivations.

Note that we do predict that the above situation will never arise in the case of rules of reduplication and infixation, for they cannot be simply encoded into boundaries. A + boundary reduplication should never follow a # boundary rule. Again crucial data are very hard to come by.

Though the morphology of the forms of (52) is not problematic, the phonology is. The words of column (a) have the same stress as their bases, as is predicted by the fact that # blocks cyclic stress rules. However, this is not true of the words of column (b), where the main stress is on the portion following the #, and the stress of the base is reduced to 3. A tempting solution is to reduce the # boundary on the cycle at which the + boundary is first scanned. This would account for the (a) items (where there would be no cycle on the affix) and the (b) items (where the rules would apply cyclically on the stem and second affix), the cycle being blocked on the first affix by the boundary, which, because it is erased by the last affix, does not block the cycle there. However, as Alan Prince pointed out to me, this entails that a word like *standard#ize+ation*, which would have on the last cycle the form *standard+iz+ation*, be treated on that cycle exactly like *improvis+ation*, which has no boundary adjustment. However, this is not so. In *impró.visátion*, on the *ation* cycle, after stress is placed on *át*, two further things happen. The Stressed Syllable rule places a stress on *óv* (two back from a 1 stress) and the Explanation rule (which reduces a 1 stress which immediately precedes a 1 stress and is separated from it by no more than one consonant, or *rm*) destresses *iz*, which is then reduced to *ə*. The surface form is [ímpràvəzéšən]. In *standardization*, however, the Stressed Syllable rule has not applied on the last cycle, for if it did it would produce the form [stǽndàrdəzéšən], parallel to [ímpràvəzéšən], which is incorrect. The boundary adjustment solution thus fails, because it predicts that all cyclic rules will apply on the "last cycle", whereas "in actuality" only some do.

Another solution is to simply treat *standard#ization* as two words, i.e. as a compound, as we did with *Kalamafuckinzoo*. This gives the correct output for all the forms of (52b): however, it does not accord with the facts of (52a), where the affix has in two cases no stress and in the other 3 stress (*stándardìze*). Why are the two columns not treated in a parallel fashion? Do we only invoke the Nuclear Stress Rule (in its compound version) in cases where there are two affixes? Is there something about monosyllabic affixes? I don't know. At present, then, the forms of (52) stand as an important counterexample to any known theory of English phonology, but not morphology. Formally, they are of a single type: $X\#a+b$. They are not isolated exceptions, but represent large classes of words.

4.4. Summary

In this chapter we have developed the notion of a Word Formation Rule as an operation on a base, accompanied by various conditions on the base.

The base is a word, a member of a major lexical category. Each WFR specifies the unitary syntacticosemantic class of which its base must be a member. The specification of this class contains no disjunction or negation. The base is also a fully specified phonological entity of unique form.

The operation is both syntacticosemantic and morphophonological. It specifies the semantics of its output as a compositional function of the meaning of the base, and assigns the output to a specific major lexical category in a specific subcategorization. The morphophonological operation is phonologically unique, and takes place at one of these levels in the phonological derivation of the base: the input to the phonology, between the cyclic and word-level rules, or the output of the phonology. The operation also assigns a boundary to the affix it produces. This boundary is dependent on the level of the phonology at which the morphophonological operation applies.

Conditions, both morphological and phonological, may be specified on the form of the base. Phonological conditions may be either negative or positive, and they are absolute: only items which meet the conditions may serve as bases for the WFR in question. Positive morphological conditions are different. They determine the productivity of the WFR with different morphologically specified subclasses of the base. Productivity is also equated with coherence. The more productive a rule, the more coherent its semantics (in the sense of chapter 3).

5: Adjustment Rules

5.1. The Place and Role of Adjustment

It should be possible for the phonology to process the word which is derived as the output of a WFR. However, such is not always the case. Rather, in certain instances the output of a WFR must undergo adjustment before the rules of the phonology may apply. This adjustment is performed by a class of rules which change the segmental shape of designated morphemes in the immediate environment of other designated morphemes. These rules are morphological, but in a different sense from the one we have used so far.

Up to now we have been concerned with morphology as a syntactic matter: how words are built up. But the word *morphological* is also part of the vocabulary of phonology. Traditionally, there are two different kinds of phonological alternations. First there are the alternations whose conditioning factors are totally phonetic (phonological). These alternations are the province of phonemics (with, in the American tradition, other additional strictures such as biuniqueness; cf. Chomsky (1964)). Alternations which are at least partly conditioned by other factors are subsumed under the rubric of morphophonemics. This would include alternations which are restricted to certain syntactic classes, those which have lexical exceptions or are entirely lexical (governed by individual words), and those which are morphologically governed, either in that they take place only in certain (classes of) morphemes, or in that they take place only in the environment of certain (classes of) morphemes.

As we noted in chapter 1, one of the major differences between generative phonology and earlier frameworks is that the former does not distinguish between phonemic and morphophonemic alternations (cf. Halle (1962)). Within generative phonology in its most general form, each morpheme (and phoneme) has a single underlying phonological form. The phonology is then an ordered set of rules which converts this underlying form into a surface phonetic form. This set includes rules of all the types mentioned, and rules of any one type may be interspersed with rules of other types.

Our adjustment rules comprise a small class of those which were previously termed morphophonemic, namely those which are restricted to specific morphemes and take place only in the environment of specific morphemes. The claim of this chapter is that these rules may be isolated from the rest of the phonology and ordered before it.

The goal of this chapter is then twofold: both to establish the reality of the class of phenomena which have been grouped under the head of adjustment, and to show how adjustment interacts with the conception of Word Formation Rule which was elaborated in the last chapter.

We will distinguish two sorts of adjustment rules: *truncation* and *allomorphy*. A truncation rule deletes a designated stem-final morpheme before a designated suffix. A rule of allomorphy adjusts the shape of a designated morpheme or class of morphemes in the immediate environment of another designated morpheme or morpheme class. I will attempt to provide independent justification for each type.

5.2. Truncation Rules

A truncation rule deletes a morpheme which is internal to an affix, in the following general manner:

(1) $[[\text{root} + A]_X + B]_Y$
$\quad\quad 1 \quad\quad 2 \quad\quad 3 \;\to\; 1\; \phi\; 3$
where X and Y are major lexical categories

All the rules of truncation which I have found in English apply exactly like the above schema; that is, they apply before suffixes, and only with + boundary affixes. I know of no general reason which would explain this, and the restrictions may well be accidental as far as I am concerned, and as far as our theory predicts.

5.2.1. +ee

Truncation rules are necessary within our theory simply because without them we often find cases of regularly derived words, semantically transparent, formed with affixes which we know to be alive and regular in their operation, which on the surface do not appear to have been derived from words. I will give an example. Consider the English suffix +*ee*, which was discussed briefly above. As Siegel (1971) notes, this suffix regularly attaches to verbs which are both transitive and take animate objects,[1] as with *presentee*, *employee*, and *payee*. Thus Siegel states the following rule of +*ee* Attachment:

(2) +*ee* Attachment
$[[\;\;]_V \quad\quad \text{ee}]_N$
+transitive
+animate object

Siegel notes, however, that there are a number of nouns in +*ee* which do not conform to the rule as stated. These are paired with, and presumably derived in some way from, verbs of the form *Xate*:

(3) nomin*ate*   nomin*ee*
evacu*ate*   evacu*ee*

Here the suffix +*ee* does not appear attached to any verb, but rather to the root of that verb, which can be obtained by deleting its last morpheme. Within a word-based theory of mor-

---

[1] +*ee* used to attach to verbs which took animate indirect objects as well. This condition is now obsolete, though the forms still exist. Exceptions to the general case are *escapee, refugee, devotee, absentee, standee*.

phology, such an attachment is impossible. Words of this sort would therefore seem to constitute very strong counterevidence to our theory, for though we know that *+ee* is a legitimate affix and that it is attached by a WFR, in this case the base is not a legitimate entity.

This problem is easily circumvented. All we need to do is to invoke a truncation rule of the form of (1), which operates after the WFR of (2). *+ee* will then attach to *Xate*, giving *Xate+ee*, which is legitimate in our theory, and subsequently *ate* will be removed from between *X* and *+ee*, giving us the form *Xee*[2] that is the input to the phonology. But simply invoking a rule of the form of (1) is not enough. We must show that it does something else than save our theory.

How do we handle a word like *evacuee* without a rule of truncation? Siegel's solution is to modify (2) as follows:

(4)   *+ee Attachment (revised)*
   a. as (2)
   b. $[[\ ]_X ee]_N$
      where there exists Y_V
                     +transitive
                     +animate object
      such that $[Y]_V = [[\ ]_X\ ]_V$

There are several disadvantages to this solution which the previous one, utilizing (2) and truncation (1), does not have. In the following discussion of their relative merits, we will call the solution of (4) A and the other B.

   I.   B allows us to state the WFR as one rule. A forces us to bifurcate the WFR itself. Formally, (4a) and (4b) are two distinct and unrelated rules. If we want to establish some connection between them stating that we are dealing with the same affix, then we must invent some new mechanism (the nature of which I cannot really speculate on) to express this relatedness between rules. Our theory is of course built on a very strict "one affix, one rule" basis, permits only solutions of the form of B, and therefore avoids the extra mechanism. Apart from formal matters, there is the problem that (4a) fails to operate just in the places where (4b) operates. *Evacuatee* and *nominatee* are evidence of this disjunction. Within A we need an independent restriction on (4a) to the effect that it does not operate in the places where (4b) does. Of course no such restriction is needed within B. This will always be the case. Solutions of the B type will always entail a disjunction of surface types, which solutions of type A will always be forced to state independently and ad hoc.

   II. A utilizes a labeled bracket $[\ ]_X$ in (4b). The label on this bracket has no significance external to the rule (4b). We must resort to it arbitrarily, in order to express the fact that *Xee* is an analyzable entity. Within B, there is no recourse to be had to arbitrary brackets. To the extent that we wish to rid any theory of arbitrary brackets, B is the more highly principled solution, for descriptions of this type *never* entail the use of other than syntactically motivated bracketing.

[2] The word *dedicatee* is an exception to the rule. We might trace its exceptionality to the fact that because of English spelling the *c* of *dedicee* would undergo the $k \to s$ rule, giving the surface form [dedisi:].

III. The condition on (4b) is strange. It says that we may have one word if there exists another from which it is not, strictly, derived. We have seen instances in which we may *not* have a given word if there exists another, and these were attributed to the blocking rule of the lexicon, which is a convention on slot-filling. However, the case at hand, which is positive rather than negative, can have nothing to do with the blocking rule. In fact, the only examples of such constraints as that on (4b) arise in cases where we could alternatively use a solution of the form B, which uses truncation, instead of the condition. Since truncation has more uses than the mere encoding of this constraint, and accommodates it incidentally and necessarily, a solution which uses truncation is to be preferred.

We see then that solution B enjoys several advantages over solution A. Solution A has only the merit of not necessitating a truncation rule. However, since it is the truncation rule itself which is the source of the advantages of B, we must suspect this latter advantage. Note that the desirable qualities of truncation exist completely apart from our theory of WFRs.

5.2.2. +ant

The advantages of I, II, and III, which a solution using truncation enjoys over one which does not, are very general ones. They will be evident in all cases. This next case, which is little more complex, shows us another sort of advantage of B over A, which will not always be evident.

A class of words closely related to those in +*ee* is that of nouns ending in the suffix +*ant*, such as *lubricant* and *complainant*. +*ant* can be said to be in some sense the active equivalent (not quite) of +*ee*. Words in this suffix fall initially into two classes: those which have some morphologically related verb (*complainant/complain, lubricant/lubricate*), and those whose roots are not free words (or cannot be related by truncation to free words) (*merchant, penchant, pedant*). We will disregard the second group, which is not interesting for our purposes, and concentrate on the first, those with related verbs. This class is further subdivided into two classes:

(a) Those items whose related verb is of the form $X+ate$, such as *officiant* and *negociant*.
(b) Those whose related verb is unsuffixed, such as *descendant* and *complainant*.

There is only one exception to this bifurcation: *deodorant*, which is related to the verb *deodorize*. Class (a) is of course morphologically unique, marked by the final morpheme +*ate*. It is the one morphological type which is especially productive with the suffix +*ant*. (Thirty-two of the 95 items in Walker (1936) which are in classes (a) or (b) are in class (a), a very high number for a single morphological class.) It is also semantically coherent, as expected by our general association of productivity and coherence.

Now, there are two ways to state the +*ant* rule, corresponding exactly to the two ways we had to state the +*ee* rule. We will again refer to the solutions as A and B, where B refers to the solution which utilizes a rule of truncation, and where A uses two WFRs instead (one for the (a) cases, and one for the (b) cases). All the arguments I, II, and III of section 5.2.1 apply in this case, in favor of the B (WFR plus truncation) solution. In addition, however, we have to encode the productivity fact, something which did not arise in the case of +*ee*. Within the B solution, the productivity of class (a) (*X*+*ate* base) is no problem, for the WFR precedes the truncation rule, which happens to remove the relevant environment for the statement of the productivity. In solution A, however, words of the form *X*+*ate* only show up in a condition on a WFR (... where there exists a word of the form *X*+*ate*...) as in (4b). We have correlated productivity with the morphology of the base; moreover, we have found a simple way to express this fact within a theory which uses word-based WFRs, and we see now, crucially, truncation rules. Without truncation rules, this whole system falls apart, for what we take to be the defining morpheme of the productive class of bases never appears in a WFR itself, but only in an ancillary condition on one.

There is additional evidence here in favor of the truncation solution, evidence in the form of exceptions. From *inflate* and *dilate* we expect to have the words *inflant and *dilant, instead of which we get *inflatant* and *dilatant*, seemingly contrary to the truncation rule. However, these exceptions can be easily explained. There is a constraint in English against nonsyllabic roots. If +*ate* were a suffix with the two verbs in question, then they would have the following morphological forms:

(5) in=fl+ate   di=l+ate

This gives us the roots */fl/ and */l/, which we know on independent grounds to be impossible. Therefore, (5) is the wrong representation for the verbs, and it must rather be (6):

(6) in=flate   di=late

But then -*ate* is not a morpheme, for it has no boundary; that is, it is not +*ate*. Therefore, truncation, which is defined as applying only to morphemes, will not apply here.

It is important to note that these exceptions are not isolated. The same thing happens with the truncation of +*ate* before +*able*.[3] Normally, +*ate* truncates here as in (7):

(7) relegate   relegable
     penetrate   penetrable
     consecrate   consecrable

However, with the verbs of (6) this is impossible:

(8) inflate   *inflable   inflatable
     dilate   *dilable   dilatable

Because all truncation is restricted to morphemes, there is no need to note these exceptions in any way within a theory incorporating rules of truncation. However, within a theory which does not have truncation rules, some other means must be found to encode this generality. Within A, the only way is to put a restriction on the conditions on rules of the form (4b). Since this restriction is completely ad hoc within theory A, we are led to prefer the theory which utilizes truncation, for in that theory we need no unprincipled restriction at all.[4]

---

[3] Truncation takes place only before +*able* and not before #*able*. Cf. chapter 6 for further discussion.

[4] I am arguing ahead of myself here. As defined, Truncation intrinsically follows all WFRs.

5.2.3. Comparative +er

For those who are beginning to suspect some intimate connection between truncation and the suffix +*ate*, I provide this last and most striking case, which has to do with the adverbial suffix *ly* and the comparative suffix +*er*.

Except in a few suppletive cases, the comparative of adjectives may be formed in two distinct ways:

(a) The suffix +*er* is attached to the adjective, as *big/bigger, small/smaller*.
(b) The independent word *more* is placed in front of the adjective, as in *more interesting*.

The choice between (a) and (b) is determined phonologically. Monosyllables, and disyllables ending in *y*, take (a) (*stupider* and *apter are exceptions); all others take (b). Some disyllables in *y*, namely those which can be analyzed as *X+ly*, take either (a) or (b). The following table illustrates the various restrictions:

(9)
adj	more adj	adj-er
big	*more big	bigger
fast	*more fast	faster
happy	?more happy	happier
silly	more silly	sillier
lovely	more lovely	lovelier
sprightly	more sprightly	sprightlier
comely	more comely	comelier
perverse	more perverse	??perverser
flagrant	more flagrant	*flagranter
pompous	more pompous	*pompouser

Turning to adverbs, we observe that monosyllables take +*er*:

(10) He ran fast/faster/*more fast today.

(11) He ran slow/slower/*more slow yesterday.

Most disyllabic and longer words take *more*:

(12) He did it skilfully/*skilfullier/more skilfully.

Disyllables of the form $C_0VC_{0\,A}+ly_{Adv'}$, that is, those formed from adjectives by the regular adverb rule, are odd:

(13) a. I am strongly inclined to believe it.
    b. I am more strongly inclined to believe it.
    c. I am stronger inclined to believe it.

(14) a. He ran quickly (*quick).
    b. He ran more quickly.
    c. He ran quicker.

(15) a. He spoke softly (*soft).
　　 b. He spoke more softly.
　　 c. He spoke softer.

The (a) and (b) forms in each of the paradigms are expected; the (c) forms are not. If +*er* were attached to disyllabic adverbs ending in *y*, as it is to such adjectives (cf. (9)), then we would expect the forms **stronglier*, **quicklier*, **softlier*, which are not only nonoccurring, but also impossible. The simplest and most elegant solution to the problem is to formulate a truncation rule which operates only on the class of adverbs in question.

(16)　*Adverb +er Truncation*:
　　　$C_0 V C_0$ +ly+er$_{Adv}$
　　　　1　　2　3 →
　　　　1　　ϕ　3

By using the truncation rule (16), which is ordered after WFRs like all truncations, we allow ourselves to state exactly the same conditions on the distribution of +*er* and *more* for adverbs and adjectives. The only difference between the two classes is the operation of rule (16) in the former, though not in the latter.

No other solution is unproblematic. If deletion (truncation) applies before the WFR, more or less as in an A solution, the conditions for +*er* attachment are met (monosyllables); but, in order to permit the derivation of the (b) forms as well, we must somehow make the deletion optional. We then cannot capture the parallel between the present instance of being allowed to form two comparatives, and the corresponding instances in (9). This is the +*ant* problem in another guise. In addition, if we delete before the comparative rule applies, what is the category of the item we form the comparative from? If from *softly* we go through *soft* to *softer*, is this *soft* an adjective, as it should be if the *ly* rule is to have any validity? But, if it is an adjective, then do we form the comparative of an adverb in these cases from an adjective? And, if it isn't an adjective, then what is it? -- for it is clearly not an adverb. This is the problem of the label (II) of section 5.2.1 in another guise.

We see then that not only does the solution which incorporates a truncation rule avoid all the difficulties which are attendant on other solutions in the case at hand, it also allows us to express a generalization of some interest and to collapse the comparative-forming rules for adjectives and adverbs.

Alan Prince has pointed out to me that substantially the same situation holds for superlatives as for comparatives, and that we might wish to extend the truncation solution to those forms as well, in which case truncation of *ly* would take place before a class of morphemes rather than before a single morpheme.

He has also noted that the truncation is restricted syntactically. Only the *more* form occurs before an adjective:

(17)　more deeply philosophical
　　　*deeper philosophical
　　　more frankly phony
　　　*franker phony

Since I have not looked at conditions on truncation rules, I cannot really comment on the import of this case. It is an open question at present whether comparative formation itself is a syntactic or derivational phenomenon. If it is syntactic, then it does not strike me as odd that the specification of the form of the comparative should depend on the syntactic environment of the compared adverb. But this must await further investigation.

5.2.4. TruncaWFRs

One simple way to avoid truncation altogether is to build truncation processes into WFRs. This is at first not implausible. As we have seen, it seems likely that for languages like Hebrew at least, WFRs must be powerful enough so that they can not only add phonological material, but also replace one piece of phonological material with another (replacing vowel patterns). If WFRs need to do this anyway, then we must question the necessity of truncation rules. We could, for instance, have +*ant* simply replace +*ate*, and *ruminate* would become *ruminant* in one step.

The answer to this suggestion lies in the "one suffix, one rule" ethic. If we allow a WFR to do the work of a truncation rule in this or any other case, we will need a separate WFR for each morphological subclass of the base where truncation operates. In this case we need two +*ant* rules, one which truncates, and one which does not. We then run into the problem of how to relate the rules, a problem which, as noted above, truncation avoids by its very essence.

The "one suffix, one rule" ethic is the same as the unitary base hypothesis. Truncation rules serve the same function as does the separate statement of morphological conditions on the base. We are trying to extract a central core for each rule, which will be uniform and will not vary with morphology. The various peripheral devices are then called upon to adjust this ideal situation to the vagaries of reality. This is the prime motivation behind the separation of the various types of rules. Of course, mere esthetic motivation is not sufficient; we must have empirical confirmation of the merit of our system. This I have tried to provide.

5.2.5. Truncation and Phonology

Though truncation as a process does not resemble greatly any phonological rule type that I am aware of, one must still ask what the relationship is between the two, as we did with WFRs. As far as I can tell, truncation rules, like WFRs, never have to be ordered among phonological rules. All the cases I have found, which involve + boundary affixes, can be ordered before all phonological rules. Some Russian examples are discussed below, in one of which a truncation rule interacts with the phonology. There, we seem to be dealing with a # boundary affix, which triggers truncation of the last morpheme of the base, but not until the cyclic rules have been applied to the base. If this is indeed what is going on in this case, we can correlate the place of the truncation rule in the phonology with the boundary of the affix before which truncation takes place. The ordering of truncation rules with respect to the phonology would then exactly correspond to that of WFRs, which, as we noted, is a function of boundaries. The problem is that in order to establish the validity of the Russian example, a much greater knowledge of Russian phonology is needed than I have at present. Even in the light of the Russian case, it is clearly possible to claim that truncation is not a phonological process, in the same way we claimed that WFRs were not phonological, while at the same time maintaining that truncation rules are not WFRs. Truncation rules will now be intrinsically ordered after WFRs, and will enjoy (probably, though the evidence is scanty) the same ordering with respect to the phonology that these latter do.

5.2.6. Russian Truncation

The truncation mechanism proposed above is not novel. Though I know of no explicit mention of such a mechanism within the scant modern work on English morphology, there is at least one very thorough discussion of truncation in the literature. This is an article in Russian by A. V. Isačenko (1972), whose title translates as "The Role of Truncation in Russian Word Formation".

Many of the truncation phenomena which Isačenko discusses are strikingly similar to those I have found in English (as indeed the case should be if there is any real significance to the device). Because of this coincidence, and because Isačenko's work may not be readily accessible to the reader of this monograph, I give below a brief summary, with comments, of the relevant examples.

Isačenko discusses various truncation rules which prevent surface suffix doubling. For example:[5]

$$\{ov\}_1 + \{ov\}_2 \rightarrow \{ov\}_2 : \begin{cases} (suvor+ov) + (ov+, \#c) \} \rightarrow suvórovec \\ (roz+ov) + (ov+at) \} \rightarrow rozovátyj \end{cases}$$ (yj is an inflectional ending.)

Structurally, this rule is very similar to an English rule discussed below:

(18) *Truncation*
$$X+ate_V+At+ivn_N$$
$$1 \quad 2 \quad 3 \quad 4$$
$$1 \quad \phi \quad 3 \quad 4$$

First, $X+ov$, like $X+ate$, need not be semantically decomposable; that is, X need not occur as a free stem. Second, it is the first occurrence of the suffix which deletes.

A second rule of double suffix truncation involves the suffix $\#sk$, by which *leningrádskij* is derived from *leningrád*. When a stem is of the form $X+sk$, as in *tómsk*, truncation takes place: *tómskij/*tómskskij*. It is important to note in connection with this rule that not all Xsk roots allow truncation. So, for example, we find *básk/báskskij*, not *básk/*báskij*. From data such as these, Isačenko concludes that only morphemes truncate and that *bask* is monomorphemic. It has already been seen, in the case of the exceptional behavior of forms such as *inflate/inflatant/*inflant*, that the same holds of English truncation rules: only morphemes truncate.

Isačenko stresses the importance of semantic evidence. Often one form is based on another not only formally, but semantically as well. Within a word-based theory, truncation rules allow us to express these semantic regularities. Isačenko gives two particularly elegant

[5] The transcription and notation are Isačenko's in all the Russian examples cited below. In particular, # stands for the vowel(s) commonly termed *yer*; it is not a boundary.

examples of the use of truncation to capture semantic facts. These examples also involve phonological evidence of a type which I have not found for any English truncation rule, but which further search will hopefully reveal.

The first case has to do with truncation of the adjective suffix #n in deadjectival verbs, whose semantics may be roughly described as V = 'make (self) adj.' For example:

(19) oburžuázit, 'make bourgeois' vs. buržuáznyj 'bourgeois'

Unless we derive the verb from the adjective, and subsequently truncate the #n before the verbalizer (it, or et,), we cannot express the semantic facts in a simple manner. In many cases the adjective in question is related to a noun, from which one might wish to derive the verb; no truncation rule would be necessary if this were done, since the noun consists of the bare stem, without the adjective marker #n. Isačenko shows that in several instances such a derivation is phonologically impossible.

For example, the adjective sekrétnyj 'secret' is formed from the noun sekrét 'secret'. One might be tempted to derive the verb zasekrétit, directly from the noun, obviating the truncation rule. However, in a case like cyngótnyj$_{Adj}$/cyngá$_N$ 'scurvy$_{Adj/N}$', the verb (cyngótet, 'become ill with scurvy') cannot be derived phonologically from the noun. This is evidence for using the truncation rule in all cases.

The second such case has to do with verbs with the following form:

(20) o+bez+N + verbalizer (obezumet,)

Such verbs are traditionally derived from the phrase bez N 'without N' and are semantically characterized as V = 'make Nless'; thus bez umá 'without a mind', obezúmet, 'make mindless'. Isačenko argues that such a derivation is incorrect, and that the verb is derived rather from the adjective bez+N +#n (here bezúmnyj), the #n adjective ending being truncated in the same way as in the case discussed above. Isačenko presents three pieces of phonological evidence to support his contention. These can be extracted from the following paradigm:

(21) bez N 'without N'   bez+N+#n$_A$ 'Nless'   o+bez+N+verbalizer$_V$ 'make Nless'
   a. bez umá 'mind'   bezúmnyj   obezúmet,
   b. bez lóšadi 'horse'   bezlošádnyj   obezlošádet,
   c. bez vredá 'harm'   bezvrédnyj   obezvrédit,
   d. bez vodý 'water'   bezvódnyj   obezvódit,
   e. bez zemlí 'land'   bezzemél,nyj   obezzemélit,
   f. bez nadéždy 'hope'   beznad,óžnyj   obeznad,óžit,

(I) The first piece of evidence is of the same sort as the last case. In (21f), the vowel e of the noun corresponds to o of the adjective. The verb has the same vowel as the adjective, and thus must be derived from it, for phonological reasons.

(II) Second, the place of the stress, which is unpredictable on the noun, is constant on the adjective (predesinential). The verb has the same stress as the adjective. Since the stress of verbs with the verbalizing suffixes i and e is not usually predictable, one must derive the verb from the adjective.

(III) Finally, in (21e) there is a complex phonological connection between the noun and the adjective. This is because of the presence of *yers* (represented by #) in the stem /zem#l,/ and the suffix /#n/. # vocalizes before a syllable containing another #, otherwise it drops.[6] So /bez+zem#l,+#n+yj/→/bezzemel,nyj/. (The first # vocalizes and the second deletes.) The second *yer* provides the crucial environment for the vocalization, and vocalization must precede deletion. In the corresponding noun, since there is only one #, the vocalization rule cannot apply, and this #, which was vocalized in the corresponding adjective, is deleted: *zeml,a*. However, in the verb, which like the noun should have only one underlying # (that of the root), this # is unaccountably vocalized. Unaccountably, that is, unless we derive the verb from the adjective. The # of the adjective suffix will cause the # of the root to vocalize, and the suffix will be deleted via the familiar truncation rule. The derivation of the verb is given below:

(22) *Input 1*   bez+zem#l,+#n$_A$
                       e   # Vocalization
                       é   Stress
                       ϕ   # Deletion
     Output 1   bezzemél,+n$_A$
                 o+*output 1* + it,   WFR
                 obezzemél, + it,   Truncation

There is no other plausible way to produce the correct surface reflex of the # in the verb. An example such as this provides the strongest sort of evidence possible for the existence of truncation rules. As I have already noted, I have not been able to find such strong evidence in English, but the similarity of the English truncation rules to those which are posited for Russian, as well as the existence of this evidence for the Russian rules, provides indirect support for the positing of the truncation mechanism as a general one and thus provides support for a word-based theory of morphology. We see that this is so because, as I have stressed, it is only in this type of theory that the truncation mechanism is necessary, and it is only in this theory that truncation rules must follow Word Formation Rules.

5.2.7. German ge- Deletion

Not all rules which delete specified morphemes are rules of truncation. In order to be a rule of truncation, a rule must have an entirely morphological environment. A rule which deletes a specific morpheme, but in a phonological environment, is not a rule of truncation. An expected consequence of this differentiation is that the latter sort of rule can be ordered among the rules of the phonology, for it is a phonological rule. We will give an example: the rule which deletes the prefix *ge-* in German past participles. We will discuss this rule as formulated by Kiparsky (1966).

---

[6] I have glossed over the problem of the # vowel. Isačenko notes that this vowel must be deleted before the truncation rule applies. Such an ordering is not possible within a theory which sharply separates truncation rules from the phonology. The whole depends on the reality of the # vowel. Its existence is supported by Halle (1973b) but not by the general theory of Kiparsky (1973), for # is a forbidden abstract segment. If we accept Kiparsky's position, then the rule deleting # is no longer a problem, for it cannot exist.

In German, past participles normally have the prefix *ge-*, when the first syllable of the participle is stressed. Otherwise *ge-* does not appear. However, there is a class of exceptions to this simple generalization. Consider the following two sets of participles, both of which are verbs in the inseparable prefix *miss*:

(23) a. missfállen, missbráucht, missbílligt
 b. míssverstànden, míssgestàltet, míssinterpretìert

According to our simple statement of the distribution of *ge-*, it should show up on the participles in (23b), since the stress in these cases falls on the first syllable. Kiparsky solves this problem by a judicious ordering of independently motivated rules. He notes that the prefix *miss-* is itself stressed only before an unstressed stem syllable, as in (23b), in which case the stress on the stem itself is reduced by general convention. If we hypothesize that the absence of *ge-* in (23b) is determined before the stressing of *miss-*, i.e. between the rule that gives the stem stress and the rule which stresses *miss-*, then we can preserve the generalization that *ge-* does not appear before unstressed initial syllables, since the *miss-* in the items in (23b) is not stressed until after the *ge-* distribution is established.

Note that if we posit a rule of *ge-* Deletion, a rule which deletes a specified morpheme, then this rule is ordered between two phonological rules: the rule which stresses the stem and the rule which stresses *miss-* before an unstressed stem syllable. If *ge-* Deletion were a rule of truncation, then this ordering would constitute a counterexample to our general claim that rules of truncation cannot be ordered among phonological rules. However, consider the condition under which *ge-* deletes: before an unstressed syllable. This is not a morphological condition, but rather a phonological one. Therefore, *ge-* Deletion is not a rule of truncation and hence is no counterexample to our general claim.

I have adduced this example because I wish to make it clear what the extent of the ordering claim is with regard to truncation rules. As we have formulated the notion, not all rules which contain morphological information are rules of truncation or allomorphy. Only those rules which delete specific morphemes in the context of other specific morphemes are truncation rules. I am claiming that these specific rules are ordered before all the rules of the phonology. I am making no claims with regard to other rules which may be similar to these in certain respects. The ordering of a rule such as *ge-* Deletion is not predicted in any way by the theory of truncation rules being presented here.

5.3. Allomorphy Rules

A rule which effects a phonological change, but which only applies to certain morphemes in the immediate environment of certain other morphemes, we will call a rule of allomorphy. We will claim that such rules are external to the phonology in the same way that truncation rules and WFRs are.

An important restriction on the power of rules of allomorphy is that they cannot introduce segments which are not otherwise motivated as underlying phonological segments of the language. This of course makes them very different from rules of the phonology. It also places a rather strong constraint on a powerful device. Unconstrained rules of allomorphy are the most powerful means of expressing phonological alternations available. They are capable of encoding all types of behavior, exceptional and regular, and do not differentiate between the various types. The ordering of allomorphy rules before the rules of the phonology, strict limitations on the environment in which these rules may operate, and the restriction to underlying phonological segments, greatly constrain this otherwise omnipotent device.

Allomorphy rules are different from truncation rules in that the former look like phonological rules, while the latter do not. Our first task is thus to isolate allomorphy rules from phonological rules. The major claim to be made in that regard is that rules which have the formal property of being restricted to certain designated morphemes, in the immediate environment of certain other designated morphemes, are always outside (previous to) the phonology. We then see that, in their restriction at least, allomorphy rules are the same as truncation rules, and that they have the same ordering properties with respect to the rest of the grammar. We therefore group them together as rules of morphological adjustment.

In accord with the order of tasks, we will first provide a relatively detailed account of certain problems which arise if we attempt to give a detailed analysis of English nouns of the form *Xion*. We will show how these problems can be solved by positing a class of rules of allomorphy. Then we will see how these rules fit into our general theory of word formation and morphology.

5.3.1. ion

This section is a detailed study of the English suffix +*Ation* and its variants, and of the variation it conditions. We will refer to the suffix as *ion*, but this is merely for typographical convenience. The basic form of the suffix we will suppose to be +*Ation*; this is the form inserted by the WFR of *ion*.

The suffix is very widespread and productive. Walker (1936) lists about 2,000 words ending in it, comprising a total of approximately 4% of the words listed in that dictionary. In its active use as a WFR, *ion* is a deverbal abstract action nominal suffix, with both active and passive senses (*fascinate/fascination, relegate/relegation*). The semantics and syntax of the suffix are very interesting; however, we will not concern ourselves with these here. We will include in our study nominals whose stems are not free words (*compunction/*compunct, salvation/*salve* (on this reading)). We will also include the very few *ion* nominals whose bases are adjectives or nouns instead of verbs (*contrition/contrite, ideation/idea*).

Note that not all instances of orthographic -*ion* are to be taken as instances of the suffix *ion*. This includes all forms in which the *i* is syllabic (*dandelion, accordion, ganglion*), as well as words like *onion, companion,* and *million*, which can probably be excluded on semantic grounds. The exclusion of these latter forms is not crucial to our argument, however. According to our theory of WFRs, they can be analyzed as words with the same status as a word like *possible*, and they probably are so analyzed by the majority of people, though their etymology shows them to be otherwise derived.

The regular phonology of the suffix is dealt with very convincingly in SPE. There it is given the underlying phonological form (+*At*)+*iVn*, where V stands for an indeterminable lax vowel that we will represent by *o*. +*ion* must be bisyllabic because of stress behavior, namely the placement of primary stress on the syllable preceding it (*prohibition* (SPE, 87)), and the operation of trisyllabic laxing on the immediately preceding vowel (*decide/decision* (SPE, 182)). A later rule changes *i* to *y* (SPE, 225-227). Further rules of spirantization and palatalization yield the correct output.

5.3.1.1. Allomorphs of +Ation. As many people have noticed, the suffix +*Ation* has several different forms, as shown in (24):

(24) realize   realization   *realizion   *realizition
      educate   *educatation   education   *educatition
      repeat   *repetation   *repetion   repetition
      commune   *communation   communion   *communition
      resume   *resumation   resumption   *resumition
      resolve   *resolvation   *resolvtion   resolution
                                  *resolvion

From (24) it is easy to conclude that *ion* has at least four, and possibly five, forms:

(25) +Ation, +ition, +ution, +ion, +tion

The distribution of the forms of (25) is complex, but I will describe it thoroughly and show both that it is morphologically governed and that it is determined before the operation of the phonology.

5.3.1.2. +Ation. This is the unrestricted variant. There are no conditions on its attachment, except that it is not affixed in cases where the conditions of attachment of the other variants are met. Again I must stress the importance of this disjunction, for it shows that we are dealing with variants of the same thing, and not with five different affixes and a blocking rule.

The following chart demonstrates attachment of +*Ation* to stems ending in various segments and clusters. It appears to be unrestricted, except for the matter of coronal fricatives, discussed in 4.3.4.1.

(26) *Labial*   *Coronal*   *Velar*

     perturbation   cessation   deportation   evocation
     formation   degradation   manifestation   purgation
     exhumation   elicitation   consultation   prolongation
     usurpation   accusation   affectation
                     revelation   commendation
                     declaration   sensation
                     examination   indorsation
                     representation

There are only a few instances of *+Ation* after a vowel-final stem. This fact can be traced to the fact that *+Ation* attaches only to *latinate* stems and to the paucity of vowel-final *latinate* stems. A few examples are *vary/variation, continue/continuation,* and *renounce/renunciation*. There is, however, one very interesting class of vowel-final stems that we will discuss in some detail. As noted in SPE, verbs in *+fy* and *+ply* generally have nominals in *-ication*, e.g. *amplify/amplification, imply/implication*. This rather singular alternation is covered by the following "ad hoc" rule of phonology found in SPE (201, rule 62):

(27) $k \rightarrow \phi / + C_1 \bar{i} \_\_ \#\#$

Amplify is thus derived from *amplifīk*, and the short *i* in *amplification* arises from the application of the Explanation rule, which destresses prestressed vowels. Rule (27) is ad hoc in the best sense of the word. It is so formulated as to have its structural description met only by verbs with the roots *+fy* and *+ply*. Even the + boundary does its job, preventing *dis#līk* from being converted into *dis#lī*. One peculiarity of the rule is that there is no known rule of English phonology which must precede it (Vowel Shift must follow it). We can wonder whether the rule's ordering can be attributed to any of its other peculiarities. (We will return to this case below.) Note that apart from any other of its peculiarities, a form like *amplification* is also different from those in (26) in that the *ion* nominal does not include the free form of the verb. We will look at a similar case, one in which, though we can motivate the unrestricted variant form *+Ation*, there is no simple agglutination on the surface (or at the underlying phonological level) because of the intervention of a truncation rule.

5.3.1.3. *Stems of the Form* X+ate. Verbs of the form *X+ate* (*equivocate, prevaricate*) form one of the most productive base classes for the *ion* rule, rivaled only by the base form *X#ize* (*communalization*). As Siegel (1971) notes, in the nominal derived by *ion*, one finds only one *At*, instead of the expected two: *equivocate/equivocation/*equivocatation*. This is quite general (the only real exception is *dilatation* from *dilate*).[7] This fact can be accounted for by a rule of truncation, like those of section 5.2.

As in some of the Russian cases, we have here a truncation rule which reduces double suffixes to one. We must then question which *+At* is truncated, the first or the second, and whether it indeed matters. I have no simple answer here. Note that in all other cases of *+At* truncation, the *+At* which occurs as the first one here is deleted (*nominee, dominant, penetrable*). For reasons of symmetry, and if we wish to combine all *+At* truncations in one, we might like to delete the first *+At* here, which, as noted, corresponds to the one deleted elsewhere. On the other hand, there is some very complex evidence from Brame's (1972a) analysis of words of the form *X+At+ory*, that it is the second *+At* which must truncate. I will not go into Brame's evidence here, but if he is correct,[8] then we must opt for a different truncation rule here than in other cases of *+At* truncation.

[7] Truncation does occur in *relation, inflation*, and similar cases, where it does not occur otherwise. This may be evidence in favor of truncating the second, rather than the first *+At*, as Brame's (1972a) analysis suggests.

[8] Brame's analysis here also contradicts Martin's (1972) analysis of the affix *+ory*, which she claims, with much evidence, is derived from the nominal *X+ation*.

5.3.1.4. The Marked Roots. We will now turn to the other variants of the suffix, those that are restricted to certain morphological environments. The distribution of these restricted variants is governed by *latinate* roots, of the sort discussed in section 2.1. These are true morphemes, with (as demonstrated at length in 2.1) no meaning. The form of the suffix is never determined by a specific word. It is never the case that one verb in a given root will allow one variant, and other verb in the same root a different variant. The form of the suffix is root governed, that is, morphologically governed. There are no exceptions to this. It is the first law of the root, originally discovered by the great Semitic grammarian ben-Moshe (ms) and called Ben-Moshe's First Law.

We will illustrate ben-Moshe's first law in (28) with the root *sume*. The variant of *ion* which appears after *sume* is +*tion*:

(28) subsume   subsumption   *subsumation
     consume   consumption   *consumation
     resume   resumption   *resumation
     presume   presumption   *presumation
     consume   consumption   *consumation
     assume   assumption   *assumation

Note that the form *consummation*, as in Shakespeare, is not an exception. Rather it is derived from the base *consummate*, by truncation. Note also that there is nothing phonological at work, in the conditioning at least. The root *hume*, as in *exhume*, is not restricted, and its nominal is therefore *exhumation* and not *exhumption*. Similarly for *deplume/deplumation/*deplumption*.

We have noted that the restricted variants are root governed, but we have not noted what they are. Basically there are two. For roots ending in noncoronals (that is, labials and velars), the restricted form is +*tion*; *sume* is one example of a non-coronal-final root. Others are listed below:

(29) duce   deduce   deduction
     scribe   prescribe   prescription
     ceive   conceive   conception
     deem   redeem   redemption
     sorb   absorb   absorption
     stroy   destroy   destruction

These exhaust, I think, the restrictive noncoronal roots. As we might expect, some of these are very productive morphological bases for the *ion* rule. For both *ceive* and *duce*, there exists a nominal for every verb, as documented in (30) below. One supposition which (30) dispels is that only the nonrestricted form of the affix, +*Ation*, can be productively attached. Such a supposition is actually counter to the entire theory of WFRs that we have proposed. If the variants of *ion* are indeed merely morphologically determined variants of one suffix, which they are, and if productivity is determined solely by the base of a WFR and not by the variants of the suffix, which are really not available for reference at the point of application of a WFR, then this supposition (that only the unrestricted variant can be productive), which crucially depends on the variants of the suffix to determine productivity, must be false. It is, as we see below:

(30)
receive	reception	deduce	deduction
deceive	deception	reduce	reduction
conceive	conception	seduce	seduction
perceive	perception	induce	induction
apperceive	apperception	conduce	conduction
		produce	production
		introduce	introduction
		reproduce	reproduction

The restrictive coronal roots are the most interesting and irregular class. The form of the affix after this class is not transparent. Many investigators (cf. Householder (1972), Schnitzer (1971)) have assumed it to be +*tion*, the same suffix that appears with the noncoronal roots. However, this cannot be the case; rather, the affix with this class must be +*ion*, as in SPE, for the following reasons.

First, pairs such as *rebel/rebellion* and *commune/communion* demand that we posit +*ion* at least after some liquids and nasals.

Second, as alternations like *decide/decision* and *revise/revision* argue, the vowel preceding *ion* must be laxed by the trisyllabic laxing rule. In such cases as *abrade/abrasion* and *rotate/ rotation*, this vowel has further undergone a rule which tenses nonhigh vowels in the following environment (SPE, 181):

$$/\underline{\quad} C_1^1 \begin{bmatrix} -\text{low} \\ -\text{cons} \\ -\text{back} \\ -\text{stress} \end{bmatrix} V$$

This rule also operates in alternations such as *Canada/Canadian* and *Abel/Abelian*. Crucially, there must be one and only one consonant after the affected vowel. If the suffix in *abrasion* is +*tion*, then the environment of the tensing rule is not met. There must, therefore, be a rule which deletes the *t* before the above rule applies. Since this *t*-rule has no other function and cannot be ordered after any phonological rule, the form of the suffix may as well be +*ion* after all coronals, exactly as we know it must be in *communion* and *rebellion*. Note also that the environment for the putative rule of *t*-Deletion cannot be stated phonologically, but rather must be stated in terms of certain coronal roots.

The root *vene* (*convene/convention*) shows an interesting conjunction of the matters just discussed in the two arguments above. One might be tempted to regard the alternation of this root as evidence that the suffix is +*tion* after at least some occurrences of *n*. However, if the suffix is +*tion*, then in most cases it must be deleted before the application of the tensing rule, as just shown. One would therefore have to mark *vene* as an exception to the deletion rule. The alternative way to generate *vention* (instead of the *venion* that we expect if +*ion* is attached to *vene*) is via a rule of allomorphy. I will discuss this solution below.

The other variants of the suffix are +*ition* and +*ution*. Evidence for the first is the following:

(31) add   addition
      vend   vendition
      define   definition
      X+pose   X+position
      compete   competition
      repeat   repetition
      imbibe   imbibition

The only trouble with positing another suffix in this case is esthetic. Note that previously, though we had two restricted suffixes, their environments were phonologically complementary. Because of this complementarity we might say that we have really only one restricted suffix, which attaches to verbs ending in restricted roots, and that the exact form of this suffix is subsequently determined by the phonology of the root. However, if we allow +*ition* to be a restricted suffix, we can no longer use this simple system. Roots must now not only be marked as restricted, but also for the particular restricted affix they take. We could avoid this by rather changing the form of the roots by adding *it* to them, and then having them take the appropriate restricted suffix (+*ion*). Though this latter solution is less complicated in terms of its repercussions, I see no empirical grounds for deciding between the two.

The following examples reveal the possibility that there is a suffix +*ution*:

(32) revolve   revolution
      resolve   resolution
      dissolve   dissolution
      solve   solution

The two roots are peculiar. Both end in *lv*. One could simply mark them for the restricted suffix, which in this case will be +*tion* because *v* is not a coronal. Then, a rule could change *v* to $u/\_\_t$, giving the correct output. Alternatively, we could posit a suffix +*ution* and drop the *v* instead of vocalizing it. The second solution gives us the same problems we found above with +*ition*, but again I know of no empirically relevant argument for one or the other solution.

We have established that the affix *ion* has at least three variants, an unrestricted variant +*Ation* and two restricted variants +*tion* and +*ion*, limited to bases ending in certain (not all) latinate roots. The choice between these two variants is governed by the last consonant of the root. +*tion* goes with noncoronal roots and +*ion* with coronal roots. The affixes +*ition* and +*ution* may also exist, though we will assume they do not. How are the variants assigned? By a rule of allomorphy. The rule is a little complex:

(33) Allomorphy of *ion*:

$$+Ation \rightarrow \begin{Bmatrix} +ion \\ +tion \end{Bmatrix} / X \begin{Bmatrix} +cor \\ -cor \end{Bmatrix}$$

where X α cor is one of a set of specified latinate roots

Rule (33) is a rule of allomorphy because it applies to a designated morpheme +*Ation*, in the environment of a designated set of morphemes. To my knowledge, rule (33) follows no phonological rule of English. This point is crucial. It is claimed that all rules having the form of (33) precede all phonological rules, and are not phonological rules. This claim is easily falsifiable.

5.3.2. Root Allomorphy

More striking than the allomorphy of *ion* is the fact that many of the marked roots are susceptible to allomorphy before it. This fact was first noticed by ben-Moshe and is usually known as Ben-Moshe's Second Law, though it is not really a law.

It is perfectly plausible that after the application of rule (33) determining the proper allomorph of *ion*, a word will be put into the phonology without any further adjustment. This is not always so. Let us look at two pairs:

(34)   invert   inversion [invəržən]
       insert   insertion [insəršən]

In one case we get a ž; in the same place in the other form, we find š. Both correspond to a word-final *t*. The only difference between the two pairs of (34) is that one has *v* where the other has *s*; or, stated in another way, the only difference is in their roots. No phonological rule of an orthodox type can be at work here. Note further that all *ion* nominals with roots in *vert* will show ž, and that all *ion* nominals with roots in *sert* will show š. The only plausible solution to (34) is a rule of allomorphy in at least one of the cases, which changes the root's last consonant. The simplest rule is one which voices the *t* of *vert* to *d* before *ion*. After that, well-motivated phonological rules will grind out the correct forms of (34). Note that the allomorphy rule takes place before all the phonological rules, as claimed in general.

There are other ways to produce the correct forms in (34). We could use an abstract segment t_1 which shows up as *t* everywhere except before *ion*. This sort of solution is undesirable on general grounds. We could use a rule feature, which triggers the relevant rule only when a word has the root *vert* and not when it has *sert*. But this latter solution necessitates two things; first, we are using a positive rule feature in the company of a minor rule, a rule which only applies to segments which are marked to undergo it; second, we must specify the order of this minor rule in the phonology. As it happens it is the first rule, or at least it follows no other rule. These two things are a coincidence. By using a rule of allomorphy, we are claiming that there is no coincidence, that all these things must fall together. We are simultaneously ridding our grammar of a minor rule/positive rule feature complex, a very suspect and powerful entity.

Again, let me stress that though a rule of allomorphy is formally a very powerful device, its power is highly limited by the restrictions on its use. The difference between the forms of (34) can be captured by an allomorphy rule only because of the coincidence of three features. One, the difference is morphologically governed in the strictest sense. Two, the difference can be marked prephonologically, and three, related to two, the difference can be represented by using otherwise motivated underlying segments of English. Only if these three conditions are met can we have recourse to a rule of allomorphy. The rival method of using a minor rule and positive rule feature is not so constrained, and by its very nature cannot be. Therefore the allomorphy solution, because it can be used only in this narrowly restricted type of case, is empirically more adequate.

The utility of allomorphy in cases like (34) is demonstrated. It allows us to make sense of what was previously an exception. What we will now do is survey all the marked roots and show that there are many similar allomorphy rules at work, though none so obvious perhaps as this one.

One of the problems with investigating allomorphy before *ion* is that several rules of English segmental phonology are at work in this environment and prevent us from finding the underlying allomorphs in a simple fashion. This was true in (34), where spirantization intervened and forced us to speculate a *d* in *vert*/___+*ion*. An observation of Martin's (1972) allows us to circumvent this problem. Martin notes that words in all the suffixes *ion*, *-ive*, *-ory*, and *-or* are built on the same form of a given root. If this is true, and we can assume that it is, then we can look at the relevant *-ive* or *-ory* form, where the phonology has not wreaked much havoc, to find out the underlying shape of the *ion* form, and by comparing this with the word-final form, we can discover what allomorphy is at work, if any.

I will first look at coronal-final roots, since these form the majority of roots and exhibit the most allomorphy. The table on page 107 is exhaustive and shows all possible alternations in the relevant environments.

First, we will extract what generalities we can from the whole list. Note first that of the full consonants, only *s* and *t* occur before +*ive*. The absence of any voiced full consonants before this suffix can be easily captured by the following ad hoc rule:

(35) $C \rightarrow -voice/\_\_\_+ive$

Note that there are no voiceless counterparts to *l* and *n*. If it applied to these segments, rule (35) would produce an impossible form. It is perhaps for this reason that there are no cases of *Xl+ive* or *Xn+ive*. *Rebellion* has *rebellious*, and *communion* has no corresponding adjective.

The second general fact to be noticed is that, except after *l* and *n*, +*ion* is preceded only by palatals: $\check{s}$, $\check{z}$, $\check{c}$. This is the result of palatalization, an apparently simple process (but see below and SPE (229-231)).

Another general fact to be noted is that the same form that shows up before +*ive* shows up before +*abl* in many instances. This will prove useful in one or two cases.

Looking at the alternations, we find only eight cases where the final consonant (cluster) of the bare verb is in a one-to-one correspondence (one way) with the consonant preceding +*ion* and +*ive* (disregarding (35) and palatalization). These are *Vs, Vz, st, kt, nt, nd, ns*, and *ls*. Except for *nd*, all these have exactly the same consonant before +*ive* as they do word-finally. This is the prime evidence for a phonological rule of palatalization /___+ion. The general correspondence is as in (36):

(36) $z/\check{z}$, $t/\check{s}$, $s/\check{s}$, $st/s\check{c}$

Though we would like to state this as one rule, because of its seeming generality, there are many phonological problems facing such an attempt, which I will not discuss here. Most of the

ADJUSTMENT RULES

TABLE OF MARKED CORONAL ALTERNATIONS

Sample Verbs	Verb-Final C	/+ion	/+ive
excrete, X+sert	t	š	t
X+mit (permit)	t	š	s
X+vert (convert)	t	ž	s
digest	st	šč	st
connect	kt	kš	kt
decide, explode	d	ž	s
X+cede (concede)	d	š	s
apprehend	nd	nš	ns
commune	n	n	
scan	n	nš	
convene, retain	n	nš	nt
prevent	nt	nš	nt
recense	ns	nš	
coerce	rs	rš	rs
disperse	rs	rž/rš	rs
submerge, asperge	rdž	rž	rs
adhere	r	ž	s
recur	r	rž	rs
rebel	l	l	
X+pel (expel)	l	lš	ls
convulse	ls	lš	ls
revise	z	ž	
percuss	s	š	s
admonish	š	š	t

relevant facts can be found in SPE (229-235). I will state two rules of palatalization.

(37) *Palatalization* I
     $t \rightarrow \check{c}/s \_\_\_ yV$

(38) *Palatalization* II
     $\begin{bmatrix} +\text{cons} \\ -\text{voc} \end{bmatrix} \rightarrow \begin{bmatrix} -\text{ant} \\ +\text{strid} \end{bmatrix} / \_\_\_ yV$

Turning to the one case where there is a one-to-one correspondence, but where a different consonant appears before +*ive* (and +*able*) than word-finally, we find the following:

(39) Xnd#   Xnšən#   Xnsiv#   Xnsəbl#

This is true of all the roots in -nd:

(40) fend   defend
     hend   apprehend, comprehend
     tend   pretend, contend, extend
     pand   expand
     scend   ascend, descend, condescend

nšən# tells us that the nominal/adjective stem must be either *Xnt* or *Xns*. *nsiv#* and *nsəbl#* tell us that it must be *Xns*. We may therefore posit the following rule of allomorphy:

$$(41) \quad d \rightarrow s/n\_\_\_ \begin{Bmatrix} \text{+ive} \\ \text{+ion} \\ \text{+abl} \end{Bmatrix}$$

A difference between this rule and the rule involved in the *vert/version* alternation, both of which we have called rules of allomorphy, is that this one applies to all roots of the form *Xnd*, whereas the latter applied to only one. One might wish to claim that (41) is a phonological rule rather than a rule of allomorphy, despite its odd environment. But (41) only applies in marked roots. Consider the root *mend*, as in *commend*, *emend*, *amend*, and *recommend*. This is not a marked root. It has nominals in *+Ation*: *recommendation, commendation, emendation*. If (41) were a true phonological rule, it would apply to the *+abl* derivatives of *mend* stems. But it does not: *commendable/*commensible, amendable/*amensible*. Since it does not apply to all stems of the form *Xnd* but must rather be restricted to marked roots of that form, (41) is not a rule of the phonology but a rule of allomorphy. This is an important distinction. A rule of allomorphy applies to a designated class of morphemes, and this designation should not be phonological, but rather morphological. This is true of (41).

š-final stems are curious:

(42) abolish   abolition
     admonish   admonition   admonitive
     punish   ?punition   punitive

The fact that we find *t/___+ive* shows that these stems have a nonfinal variant *Xt*. We therefore have a case in which roots show the same surface segment (š) in two environments, but where there is good evidence that these two segments must be derived from two distinct underlying segments, in different allomorphs.

t-final stems show the most varied alternations. As noted, we need an allomorphy rule for *vert*, and a glance at our table shows that the nonfinal allomorph must be *verz*, rather than the *verd* originally proposed. *mit* too is odd; it shows the form *mis* (*submissive, admissible*). Other *t*-final roots require no allomorphy. *t* remains before *+ive* and *+abl*: *assertive, transitive, excretive*.

From *vert* we can turn to other cases of *rš/rž*:

(43) coerce   coəršən   coərsiv
     disperse   dispəržən (?šən)
     immerse   imməršən (?žən)

emerge	emərž̌ən (*š̌ən)	
asperge/se	aspərž̌ən (*š̌ən)	
submerge	submərž̌ən (*š̌ən)	submərsəbl
deterge	detərž̌ən (*š̌ən)	detərsiv

It is clear that with stems in *Xerge* we always find *rž̌*. The *s* in *detersive* suggests a rule similar to that involving *nd*:

$$(44) \quad g \rightarrow z / \_\_ \left\{ \begin{array}{l} +\text{ion} \\ +\text{ive} \\ +\text{abl} \end{array} \right\}$$

Though the change is suspiciously natural, a rule of palatalization, the fact that it takes place before *+abl* should be sufficient evidence against its naturalness. Note also the back-forms *asperse* and *submerse* (*disperse* and *immerse* are also back-forms; *dispersion* is ME, *disperse* is dated 1450, *immersion* 1450, and *immerse* 1650). That these were back-formed in this way shows the opacity of (44).

The two roots in *r* are good examples of roots with their own allomorphs. One is *kur/kurz*, the other *hēr/hēz*.

Two *n*-final roots are of interest, *vene/vention* and *tain/tention*. We promised earlier to discuss the first. It should be clear by now that we derive *vention* by declaring the combinatory allomorph of *vene* to be *vent*. How does this compare with the rule which attaches *+tion*? As noted, the latter needs an exception feature, to make sure the *t* does not drop, as it presumably does elsewhere. By positing the allomorphy rule we rid ourselves not only of an exception feature, but also of the entire already suspect rule of *t*-Deletion to which *vene* is a supposed exception.

This rule of *t*-Deletion is put to use in one place in the phonological literature on the subject. Schnitzer (1971) attempts to derive *succession* from the underlying form $sub=kēd+t+iVn$. He uses the *t* to devoice the *d*. However, there is no way for him to shorten the *ē*, and his final output is *$suk=sēs+ion$. One could of course lax the *ē* before deleting the *t*, but this is not the general case (*excrētion*). We conclude that Schnitzer's use of *t*-Deletion is not valid, for it cannot lead to the proper output. In order to derive *succession*, SPE lists *cede* ($cēd$) as exempt from the tensing rule. *e* is thus shortened by Trisyllabic Shortening, and exceptionally not lengthened again. By using the device of root allomorphy, we can list *cede* as *cess* in the relevant environments. The double consonant will prevent the tensing rule from applying. Again we see that allomorphy can be a useful device for encoding an exception feature. Note that *successive* provides very strong support for our rule, for the SPE theory would derive *$succetive$, as would Schnitzer's, if it worked. One allomorphy rule can be used to cover many irregularities, sometimes irregularities which cannot be encoded as rule features at all. Nor is allomorphy a more powerful device than that of rule features. Rule features interact with phonological rules in ways in which allomorphy rules, because they are prephonological, cannot. This makes rules of allomorphy quite restricted in some respects, as compared with rule features, which can refer to any stage in a phonological derivation.

Returning to *n*-final roots, we will look at the root *tain/tent* (*retain/retention*). The *t* is clearly allomorphic. However, more interestingly, we expect not *tain/tention*, but rather *tain/*tantion*. SPE (202) accounts for this curiosity by having *tain* undergo the Short Vowel Shift rule. This is a very suspect rule. We will discuss its use in another case below and show that it is unmotivated. In fact, an inspection of all the items that this putatively general rule applies to reveals that it is a minor rule which affects only items positively specified to undergo it. Again we can use allomorphy to rid ourselves of such a rule.

d-final roots, except for *cede*, all show the same forms: *d/s/ž* (*decide/decisive/decision*). We can therefore posit a rule changing *d* to *z*. Again we must ask whether this is really a rule of allomorphy, or whether it is a phonological rule. Normally *d* does not appear before *y* (the reflex of the *i* of +*ion*) except here. In fact, the rule that changes *i* to *y* after coronals is blocked idiosyncratically by *d* in all other cases (*pavilion/enchiridion*). There is only one case where *d*+*y* arises, other than /___+*ion*, and that is in the word *cordial*, where it shows up as *dž*, presumably palatalized from *dz*. It appears, then, that this supposedly general palatalization of *d* is confined to the morphological environment in question. We can therefore account for it by a rule of allomorphy, as we would expect.

Marked noncoronals were listed in (29). They are not particularly interesting. The only real cases of allomorphy here are *stroy/struk* (*destroy/destruction*), which we noticed in chapter 2, and *ceive/cept* (*deceive/deception*).

This ends our discussion of root allomorphy. I would just like to stress the strength of Ben-Moshe's First Law here, the law of allomorphy. If a root takes a given shape in a given environment by a rule of allomorphy, then it takes that shape always. There are no lexical exceptions to rules of allomorphy, and they are a living part of a language.

5.3.2.1. fy and ply. Rule (27), as stated, is not a rule of allomorphy. This is because its environment is not totally morphological, for it is bounded on one side by #. There is a way to make the alternation expressed by (27) a morphologically conditioned one, namely to state not (27) but its reverse, a rule of *k*-insertion. I know of no deciding factor between the two.

It is of some note that a restricted form of the suffix sometimes shows up with verbs in *fy*. The only common word of this sort is *satisfaction*. Others are *putrefaction, liquefaction*, and *calefaction*; there are about ten all told. The form *fac* is derived in SPE by applying the rule of Short Vowel Shift to *fīk*, after the *i* is shortened /___CC (kt). The same case of Short Vowel Shift, incidentally, accounts for the *sing/sang* alternation. As we have noted, the rule is dubious; in any case, all these words must be idiosyncratically marked to undergo it. The concomitant irregularity of the *fak* forms – that they take +*tion* instead of +*Ation* – was not noted in SPE. Since the only difference in derivation between the *fak* forms and the regular ones is the rule feature governing the application of Vowel Shortening, presumably the choice of the affix is governed by this rule feature as well. Either that, or it is not decided until the rule in question has applied, i.e. until we can tell *fik* from *fak*. Neither system is satisfying. In the one, a rule feature governs something other than its rule – a strange situation; in the other, the form of the affix is not chosen until a late stage in the phonological derivation – a singular case, for in all others the variant of the affix is determined at the underlying level.

A simpler solution is to derive *fak* by an allomorphy rule, conditioned by the preceding morpheme (*satis, putre, lique, cale, tume, tabe, lubri, labe*), as well as by the one following (*+Ation*). In its turn, *fak* determines the variant of *ion*, namely the restricted one. This solution entails that allomorphy rules be ordered. Note, however, that the ordering is from the inside out. Though we have no other evidence, we might claim that allomorphy rules are always so ordered, in which case the ordering, though extrinsic, would not be arbitrary. However, this is not exactly a central case, and to base a broad theory on it is not advisable.

5.3.3. Other Allomorphy

Though the foregoing account of rules of allomorphy is detailed, it is based on one English paradigm, that of the suffixed forms *X+Ation*. The reader is entitled to be skeptical about a vast system which is based on one example, or even, as in this case, one phenomenon, though the phenomenon is widespread. In order for my theory to be plausible, I must find other examples of its utility. This is not so simple. One must have a good idea of what the phonology of a language looks like before proposing rules of allomorphy.

One place in which rules of allomorphy surface is in the selection of theme vowels. Such vowels are uncommon in English; however, they do appear before certain affixes. The following data are in part from SPE (129-130):

(45)
professor	professorial
manager	managerial
president	presidential
periphery	peripheral
orient	oriental
habit	habitual
tempest	tempestuous
industry	industrious, industrial
Arab	Arabian
excrement	excremental
exponent	exponential
calamity	calamitous

It is clear that there is often a difference between the unsuffixed and suffixed forms of the base. Sometimes *i* is inserted before *-al, -an,* or *-ous*, sometimes *u*, sometimes nothing. Sometimes we even find deletion of the final segment of the stem (*peripheral*). The conditions for these variations are not phonological: *periphery* contrasts with *industry*. Words ending in *ment* never have a vowel before *+al* (**departmential*), but other words ending in the same phonological sequence *-ent* sometimes do and sometimes don't (*parental/torrential, continental/ exponential*). SPE stresses that whether an item takes *i* or *u* or nothing or itself loses a segment is a property of the item itself. This determination is morphological.

In SPE, this variation is handled by assigning to each stem a stem vowel, which is dropped word-finally but shows up before suffixes. *Professor* will be entered in the lexicon as /pro=fes+Or+i/, *habit* as /hæbit+u/. The authors do not discuss forms like *peripheral*, which is presumably derived by a minor rule.

A problem for this analysis is the nominal suffix +y, which occurs in such words as *presidency*. According to the above analysis, the underlying form of *presidency* must be /president+i+y/. However, the *y* is normally vocalized to *i* by the following rule (SPE, 130):

y → i/C ___ boundary

This rule operates in such words as *industry*. Note that the presence of the stem vowel *i* in *president+i+y* will block this rule. Either there is no stem vowel before *y* in the first place, or it is deleted by a new rule:

(46) i → ϕ /___+y

The stem vowel thus shows up before some suffixes and not before others. It does not show up word-finally. In order to generate the data correctly, the SPE analysis of the forms in our paradigm needs three phonological rules in addition to the stem vowels. One rule deletes the stem vowel finally, another deletes it before +y, and a third deletes *y* in *peripheral*. These are all phonological rules. They are all, as far as I know, preceded by no other rule of the phonology.

The allomorphy solution to the paradigm is transparent. Before the suffixes in question, certain allomorphic changes take place. This step is equivalent to the marking of stem vowels in the lexicon, which is needed in any solution. Now, however, no more is necessary. We have simply incorporated the three questionable rules into the allomorphy rules, a step which simultaneously rids us of them and accounts for their ordering properties.

I think there is no question as to which is the better solution. They are both descriptively adequate; however, the SPE system is ad hoc, while the allomorphy solution, within a theory which includes rules of allomorphy, is the only possible one. It is also the correct one.

5.3.4. Allomorphy and Other Parts of a Grammar

The central import of allomorphy rules is for the phonology. By using these rules, which, it must be emphasized, are highly restricted, we are making predictions about the range of material that can be covered by rules of the phonology and about the ordering of certain "irregular" processes. It is also important to note that because rules of allomorphy are not phonological rules per se, they are not subject to many of the naturalness constraints that govern the latter. In theory, a rule of allomorphy could change *m* to *t*, something we do not expect from a rule of the phonology.

The intuition behind the positing of rules of allomorphy is quite widespread. People have felt that rules referring to morphological categories, morphologically governed rules, are ordered earlier in the system of the phonology than phonologically governed rules. Lightner (1972) argues that there is a class of minor rules characterized by the facts that (a) they always apply before all major rules, and (b) their environment always contains a reference to some morphological category. It is clear, however, that (b) is not a sufficient condition for (a). The English *k* → *s* spirantization, which is governed by the morphological feature *latinate*, is a rule of the phonology and cannot be ordered before all major rules. Allomorphy rules are finer than Lightner's rules. $k \rightarrow s$ is not a rule of allomorphy as defined, for it is governed not by a morpheme but by a morphological feature. For a rule to be a rule of allomorphy, it is a necessary and sufficient condition that it be totally morphological, in the sense defined: it applies to a morpheme, or other than phonologically designated set of morphemes, in the immediate environment of a designated morpheme or set of morphemes. This is a much narrower definition than Lightner's. Unlike Lightner's minor rules, rules of allomorphy are defined on morphemes and not segments. Also, we have narrowed somewhat our version of Lightner's (b), which would falsely include umlaut rules under the category of minor rules.

By narrowing the scope of our definition, we are of course narrowing the scope of our claim. We are not claiming that all morphologically and lexically governed rules are early rules of the phonology. We are not denying the validity of the English main stress rule, because of its baroque complexity. Phonological rules may be as baroque as they wish to be, but rules of allomorphy, as defined, will *always* precede the rules of the phonology.

A particularly fine example of a rule which, though morphologically governed, is not a rule of allomorphy and hence may be ordered among the rules of the phonology, comes from Masoretic and was pointed out to me by Alan Prince. Consider the following pairs:

(47) a. ka:*tab*ti 'I wrote'   k*tab*tihu: 'I wrote it'
     b. ka:*tab*t 'you (fem. sg.) wrote'   k*tab*tihu: 'you wrote it'

The problem is that, though the suffixed forms are identical, the unsuffixed forms differ. A relatively detailed study of Masoretic phonology reveals that the underlying forms of (47a and b) must be identical (*katab+ti*), and that *i* is deleted word finally (in second person singular feminine perfect forms *only*) at a relatively late point in the phonology, the *i* serving to block several otherwise well-motivated phonological rules which would apply to a form **katab+t*. We will formulate the rule as follows:

(48) $i \rightarrow \phi / t$ ___ #/2.f.sg. perf.

As we noted, this must be a relatively late rule of the phonology. It is a minor rule in Lightner's sense and hence should not be ordered so late in his theory. However, (48) is not a rule of allomorphy. This is because of the presence of the # boundary as the immediate environment. The morphological category, though it is crucial to the rule, is not sufficient to make (48) a rule of allomorphy. Therefore (48) may be a phonological rule in our theory; in fact, it must be, and hence it may be ordered at any point in the phonology.

Note that the reverse of (48) would insert *i* in suffixed forms of the second person feminine singular perfect and would be a rule of allomorphy. It is significant that (48), and not its reverse, is the correct rule, for in our theory the latter, as a rule of allomorphy, could not ever be ordered at such a late point in the phonology -- or anywhere in the phonology, for that matter. For those who doubt fine points, I should point out that Masoretic phonology is one of the best studied of all linguistic systems, and that the formulation of the rule in question as (48) and not its reverse has been established and accepted for centuries (cf. Gesenius (1962)).

Note the similarity between this and the German Truncation rule discussed above.

Though it applied to a designated morpheme *ge-*, this latter rule had a phonological environment; hence it was not a rule of truncation as defined and could not be ordered among the rules of the phonology. The general similarity between rules of allomorphy and rules of truncation should be apparent by now. Both types are defined on morphemes, in the environment of morphemes. The only difference is that one deletes morphemes, while the other adjusts their shapes.

Rules of allomorphy stand in exactly the same relation to WFRs as rules of truncation. Their necessity within our system of word formation is brought about by the same separation of all matters concerning the morphology of the base of a WFR from the WFR itself. In the case of rules of allomorphy, the morphology of the base both itself varies with certain affixes, and causes variation in affixes which have been introduced by phonologically constant operations. Whether both are true of truncation rules as well is not clear from the examples we have. If truncation in the forms *X+At+Ation* applies to the second *At*, which is part of the affix, and not to the first, then we have an instance of a truncation rule which applies to an affix. As noted above, however, the exact formulation of this rule is not clear.

6: Exempla

This last chapter is almost an addendum. It essentially contains no theory, but rather studies done within the theory outlined in this monograph. These studies are further characterized by the fact that they could not have been done without the underpinnings that the framework provides, and should thus serve as harbingers. The first section is purely exemplary, consisting of two cases in which distributional evidence is used to resolve a morphological quandary. Some theory does creep into the second half of the chapter; it comprises an analysis of the English suffix *-able*, making essential reference to the notions of allomorphy and truncation, but its more ulterior concern is the nature of the boundaries + and #.

6.1. Distributional Arguments

One point on which the theory of this work differs from most contemporary concepts of morphology is the claim that morphology is word-based: new words are formed from already existing ones, rather than being mere concatenations of morphemes. Now one of the more curious properties of this word-based theory is the way in which distribution can be used to test hypotheses set forth within it. Distributional evidence can be used because of the role which the lexicon plays within the theory: if one word is formed from another, then it will generally be the case that both words will be in the lexicon; the base at least will always appear there, though the derivative need not (cf. chapter 3). Therefore, if we hypothesize that a class of words X is derived from another class of words Y, then for every x_i in X there should be listed a corresponding y_i in Y, but not vice versa (unless the rule is fully productive, in which case X will not be listed anyway). There may be incidental gaps, due to the vagaries of history, but Y should by and large include X.

We will give a simple example of how this distributional test works. Consider the class of English nouns of the form $X\#ness$ (*redness, callousness, receptiveness*...). It is generally assumed that this class is derived from the class of adjectives, and there are various grounds for the assumption. For one, X is always an adjective. Second, there is the stress pattern of $X\#ness$, which demands that we posit a boundary (in this case a word boundary) before the phonological sequence [nes]. Third, there is the semantic coherence of the class of nominals, all of which carry meanings containing those of the adjectives. All of these facts are most plausibly accounted for by deriving the nouns from the adjectives they contain. We will look at the distributional evidence and see whether it is in accord with this rather strongly supported hypothesis. Consulting a dictionary, for this is the closest we can come to the lexicon of a speaker's language, we discover that for every English noun $x_i\#ness$ there exists a corresponding adjective x_i. Note that the opposite is not true; we do not find for every adjective listed in our lexicon a corresponding noun of the form $X\#ness$. Distribution thus accords with other criteria in this simple case.

But not all cases are so simple. Most WFRs are easily discernible because, like the rule of #ness, they are associated with some tangible phonetic object; there is generally a specific morpheme which is uniquely associated with a given rule. Sometimes, though, there is no such morpheme; nothing is so obviously present in one set of words and missing in another.

Consider the class of noun/verb pairs of the form $Xment$, discussed at some length in SPE and later works.

(1) | $Xment_V$ | $Xment_N$ |
|---|---|
| ornament | ornament |
| implement | implement |
| complement | complement |
| tenement | tenement |
| fragment | fragment |
| segment | segment |
| augment | augment |
| sediment | sediment |
| regiment | regiment |
| compliment | compliment |
| experiment | experiment |
| ferment | ferment |
| torment | torment |

The two classes are obviously related: there is a clear and consistent semantic relation between the pairs. But there is no morpheme which we can isolate and use to show that one class is derived from the other. There are, however, systematic phonological differences between the two classes. In the disyllables (such as *ferment* and *segment*) the verb always has final stress, while the noun has initial stress, with the [e] of [ment] being reduced to [ə].[1] In words which are trisyllabic or longer, the main stress is always on the antepenult vowel, both in the noun and in the verb, but in the noun the [e] of [ment] is reduced, as it is in the disyllabic nouns, while in the verb it is not. In order to account for these phonological differences in a principled manner, Chomsky and Halle derive the nouns from the corresponding verbs. The nouns then receive their proper stress on the application of a second cycle, which is now motivated by the morphological analysis. Chomsky and Halle note, however, that "... in the case of the forms with *-ment*... The derivation of nouns from such verbs is marginally productive, as is often the case in derivational systems of this sort" (SPE, 107, fn.). The opposite phonological derivation is impossible: there is no way to derive the stress of the verbs from that

---
[1] There are variant pronunciations of *augment*$_V$ and *segment*$_V$ which are not easily accounted for in any theory of morphology.

of the nouns. Since the advent of this phonologically motivated morphological analysis, however, Kean (1974) has proposed a very general constraint on the application of phonological rules, the principle of strict cyclicity, which directly prohibits the phonological derivation proposed in SPE. Furthermore, there has been much criticism of other sorts directed against the SPE solution (Ross (1972, 1973); Oehrle (1971)). Ross also mentions that in most cases the noun "feels" basic, though he is unable to provide tangible support for his intuition. In any case, both Ross (1972) and Halle (1973c) avoid attempting to relate the two classes phonologically in their revised analyses and simply derive them in separate ways. The phonology, then, can give us no clue to a morphological solution.

What does our distributional criterion tell us about this puzzling case? If the nouns are derived from the verbs, then we should expect to find many unpaired verbs of the form *Xment*. We find only two: *foment* and *dement*.[2] This is an admittedly small gap. Turning to the nouns, we find that Walker (1936) lists approximately 500 of the form *Xment* for which there exists no verb of the same shape. Of these, the large majority are of the form $X_V \#ment$ (*employment, dismemberment*) discussed in 4.2.1.2 and transparently derived from verbs. We may therefore exclude these nouns from our distributional computation. Apart from these, however, there still remain some 75 nouns of the form *Xment* which do not have corresponding verbs (for example, *element, figment, sediment, monument, garment*). Furthermore, all of these have exactly the same stress pattern as the nouns in (1). Distribution dictates that we account for the semantic correspondence exhibited by the pairs in (1) by a rule deriving the verbs from the nouns. We can even be nihilistic, and claim that neither set is derived from the other: the verb/noun correspondences that we do find are accidental. Whatever we choose to do, the one analysis which the distributional evidence clearly contradicts is the one in question, that of SPE, which derives the nouns from the verbs. If it were true, we would be claiming, contrary to the facts of history, that all of the unpaired nouns are derived from verbs which have somehow disappeared.

The phonological consequence of the morphological analysis is that there is no way to derive the stress of one member of the pairs in (1) from that of the other; the two classes must be independent from a phonological point of view. This consequence, however, is exactly that of strict cyclicity.[3] It is also foreseen by the stress rules of both Ross and Halle.

It is quite apparent that the morphological analysis of SPE was often grounded in phonological convenience. Here it was simpler to derive the stress of the noun from that of the verb, and hence the morphology was made to allow for that particular phonological solution. Dissatisfied with the morphological analysis, but not able to deal with it, previous investigators could take issue with only the phonological derivation, a sometimes alarmingly complex task.

---

[2] There are also pairs of words of the form *Xment* which do not differ at all in stress: *lament*$_{V,N}$, *cement*$_{V,N}$, *comment*$_{V,N}$. The stress and phonology of these words are discussed in detail in Oehrle (1971).

[3] The morphological structure of the verbs is $[[X]_N]_V$. Their stress pattern is one which is characteristically verbal (cf. Ross (1972, 1973)). It seems most plausible to assume that this pattern is arrived at by in some way ignoring the inner nominal brackets. This is not what is predicted by the strict cycle, which, admittedly was not formulated in the light of examples of this form, but rather from cases of the more usual $[[X]Y]$ or $[X[Y]]$ structure.

Distributional argumentation provides a simple and straightforward way of dealing directly with the morphological analysis. There is also a more general moral to be drawn: not to put the cart before the horse. We will now turn to a more complex case.

We will attempt to establish the derivation of the class of English adjectives of the form *Xistic* (*imperialistic, egotistic, hedonistic*), which seems transparently to be derived from the class of nouns of the form *Xist* (*imperialist, egotist, hedonist*). According to our test, if $Xist_N$ is indeed the source of $Xistic_A$, then we should find a word $x_i ist_N$ for almost every $x_i istic_A$. Walker lists 145 words of the form $Xistic_A$, for the following 28 of which he does not list a corresponding form $Xist_N$:

(2) a.   b.

a.	b.	
characteristic	solecistic	shamanistic
logistic	sufistic	eudemonistic
mediumistic	syllogistic	synchronistic
phlogistic	neologistic	anachronistic
harmonistic	catabolistic	hylozoistic
patristic	formulistic	hetaeristic
heuristic	euphemistic	poristic
eristic	animistic	euphuistic
ballistic	totemistic	humoralistic
	melanistic	

There are too many exceptions to our proposed derivation for it to be above suspicion. However, a separate fact does emerge from this list, which is that a large number of words of the form *Xistic* for which there does not exist a corresponding word *Xist* do have a corresponding word *Xism*. Testing this new possible source of $Xistic_A$, by our same method, we discover, of the total 145 words of the form $Xistic_A$, 26 which do not have a corresponding form $Xism_N$, namely those in (2a) and those in (3):

(3)
haggadistic	casuistic
talmudistic	oculistic
elohistic	stylistic
eulogistic	eucharistic
yahwistic	diaristic
annualistic	folkloristic
novelistic	juristic
artistic	linguistic
coloristic	

Quite clearly our simple distributional test has failed to give us any clear answer in this case, though it has provided us with a second plausible source for the class of words under study. The results of our inconclusive computation are tabulated in (4) and diagrammed in Figure 1:

(4) Total $Xistic_A$ 145
     $Xistic_A, Xist_N, Xism_N$ 100
     $Xistic_A, *Xist_N, Xism_N$ 19
     $Xistic_A, Xist_N, *Xism_N$ 17
     $Xistic_A, *Xist_N, *Xism_N$ 9

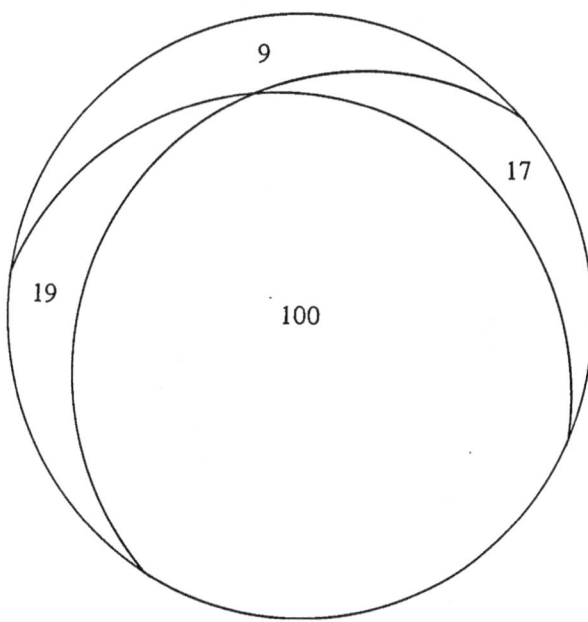

Figure 1

There is a way out of this dilemma. The way is hidden in the unitary base hypothesis of 4.1.1, according to which the base of a given WFR must comprise a unitary, positively specified syntacticosemantic class; there can be no disjunction or negation in the specification of the base. If a given class is hypothesized to be the base of a given WFR, then all members of that class must be possible token bases, and there must be no subclass of the hypothetical base class which cannot serve as a base. What we must therefore do is to look at the two classes which we have posited as possible bases for the class $Xistic$ and determine whether they meet this test. It is a distributional test, but a finer one than the first; instead of merely looking for gaps in the base, we are looking for systematic gaps.

First we will look at the class of words of the form $Xist$. This is a large class, and Walker (1936) lists about 700 words in it. Interestingly, only a small subset of these 700 allow corresponding words of the form $Xistic$. Excepting the 17^4 cases already listed in (3), the following

[4] Of the 17 gaps in Walker, the OED lists *novelism* and *folklorism*.

generalization holds:

> For a given word $x_i ist$, there cannot exist a corresponding word $x_i istic$ unless there also exists a corresponding word $x_i ism$.

This generalization is exemplified in (5):

(5)
archaeologist	*archaeologism	*archaeologistic
meteorologist	*meteorologism	*meteorologistic
alchemist	*alchemism	*alchemistic
botanist	*botanism	*botanistic
dentist	*dentism	*dentistic
symphonist	*symphonism	*symphonistic
economist	*economism	*economistic
deuteronomist	*deuteronomism	*deuteronomistic
opinionist	*opinionism	*opinionistic
extortionist	*extortionism	*extortionistic
violist	*violism	*violistic
cellist	*cellism	*cellistic
copyist	*copyism	*copyistic
lobbyist	*lobbyism	*lobbyistic
essayist	*essayism	*essayistic
reservist	*reservism	*reservistic
archivist	*archivism	*archivistic
parachutist	*parachutism	*parachutistic
balloonist	*balloonism	*balloonistic
canoeist	*canoeism	*canoeistic
latinist	*latinism	*latinistic
lichenist	*lichenism	*lichenistic

Nothing of the sort holds for *Xism*. Whether or not one can form a word $x_i istic_A$ for a given word $x_i ism$ is completely independent of $x_i ist$ (though, of course, not all members of *Xism* have corresponding *Xistic* forms). It would seem, then, that *Xism* is the base of *Xistic*, as far as distributional evidence can tell us.

Some of the examples in (5) take us beyond distribution to corroboratory evidence of a different sort. Note that the word *archaeologist* is transparently derived from *archeology*; most words of the form *Xologist* have parallel derivations. The suffix +*ic(al)*[5] attaches productively to *Xology* (*biological, meteorological, archeological*). Along the same lines we have *botanist/ botany/botanical, alchemist/alchemy/alchemical*. In fact, looking at the wider behavior of the suffix, we find that it attaches to nouns which denote inherently definite things: names of disciplines (*philosophy/philosophical, geography/geographical*), names of "concrete" objects

---

[5] The relationship between +*ic* and +*ical* is discussed with insight in Prince (1972).

(*oxygen/oxygenic*), names of people (*Napoleon/Napoleonic*), and names of languages.[6] There are some exceptions to this pattern, but they are not systematic. It is clear that nouns of the form *Xism* fall into this general class, but those of the form *Xist* do not. Now, one might claim that the base of the suffix +*ic*(*al*) departs from the unitary base hypothesis just in the instance of nouns of the form *Xist*, but to do so is surely perverse, for if the base in this case is *Xism*, uniformity is restored.

One obstacle remains in the way. The suffixation of +*ic* to *Xism* yields *Xismic* and not the desired *Xistic* (except in the case of *embolismic*). We need the following rule:

(6) m → t/s ___ +ic

This rule might also be at work in alternations such as *phantasm/fantastic, iconoclasm/iconoclastic, heteroplasm/heteroplastic, sarcasm/sarcastic*.[7] The rule also leads to an important point. The main reason for first choosing $Xist_N$ as the most plausible base of $Xistic_A$ is phonological transparency: in order to derive the latter from the former, all we do is add [ic]. What I have tried to show is that using surface concatenation (even underlying phonological concatenation) as the primary tool in doing morphology is misconceived. Word formation is a much more abstract matter than one might at first be led to believe.

To summarize this section: I have shown how a theory of word-based word formation permits us to use distributional facts of various sorts in confirming or disconfirming hypotheses within that theory. Conclusions from distribution have been supported from other quarters.

6.2. -*able*

Prima facie, this section is a study of the English suffix which is represented orthographically as -*able* or -*ible*. We will have a reasonably detailed account of its phonological properties and some observations on its semantics and syntax. A second and perhaps higher purpose of the section is to support a particular conception of the nature of morphological boundaries.

Within the theory of this work, and within the theory of SPE, boundaries are structural entities, inserted between elements by rules. Like all purely structural entities, they have no phonological substance in themselves, nor meanings in the conventional sense, but rather reveal their existence in the way in which they affect phonological and semantic processes, and, through the mediation of process, substances. The phonological reflection of a boundary is a constraint on the operation of phonological rules. The reflection of boundaries in semantic and syntactic structures is more elusive, due perhaps to the dimness of our insight in these areas. This contrast in clarity seems somehow to have led to the peculiar belief that boundaries are phonological entities. This way of thinking is revealed even in SPE, where boundaries are

---

[6] Note that of the items in (2a) and (3) which seem to be exceptions to the proposed rule, *elohistic* and *yahwistic* are not exceptions to the general case, since by definition there is only one *elohist* and one *yahwist*. Similarly, *linguistics, patristics, heuristics*, and *stylistics* are the most plausible source of their corresponding *Xistic* forms. A little rooting in the dictionary reveals that *characteristic, eristic*, and *heuristic* are borrowed or adapted directly from Greek.

[7] It may also be that the suffix is +*tic*(*al*). Evidence for this may be found in forms like *charisma/charismatic, drama/dramatic*.

analyzed, in a clearly artificial manner, into phonological features. This tendency has been aggravated in recent work, to the point where the possibility is entertained that some boundaries may be [+consonantal]. Within the framework of this monograph, such a suggestion is as sensible as claiming that NP brackets are [−continuant].

Boundaries differ in the manner in which they constrain the application of phonological rules. This difference can be seen as one of degree or strength (cf. Stanley (1973)). # is a strong boundary, and a string containing it is not subject to a phonological rule unless this rule explicitly mentions # in the proper position. + is a weak boundary; its presence can be indicated in a rule, but its absence cannot, with the result that though it can trigger rules it cannot block them. I will try to demonstrate that this difference in strength is not merely reflected in the way in which boundaries constrain phonological operations, but that it holds for syntactic and semantic operations as well. In particular, I will show that there are two suffixes, +*abl* and #*abl*, that they have the same meaning and syntactic properties, but that the consistency with which these properties appear is greater for words of the form *X#abl* than it is for words of the form *X+abl*.

If we can show that # is stronger than + with respect to phonological, syntactic, and semantic operations, then clearly boundaries cannot be merely phonological entities. Nor can they be entities of the same nature as morphemes or words. The essential property of words and morphemes is their arbitrariness; they are mediations between sound and meaning, but there can be no connection between the structure of their sound and the structure of their meaning. Boundaries have neither sound nor meaning. They affect the two in parallel manners and are therefore not elements of linguistic substance, but rather elements of linguistic structure.

6.2.1. Phonological Arguments

6.2.1.1. Stress.[8] In terms of stress, it is possible to isolate three suffixes. The most common is +*abl*, a monosyllable with a + boundary. When not followed by any further suffix, this is a final syllable with a [−long] vowel. The Primary Stress Rule (cf. Halle (1973c)) will ignore it and place stress on the penult, unless the penult is weak, in which case stress falls on the antepenult. So the word *corrigible* has a weak penult and the stress falls on the antepenult, while *refrangible* has a strong penult, which is stressed.

This analysis is contradicted in a small number of cases which show alternate stress patterns:

(7)   a.   b.
       inéxplicable   inexplícable
       hóspitable   hospítable
       éxplicable   explícable
       déspicable   despícable
       fórmidable   formídable

The stress pattern of the items in column (7a) is in accord with our hypothesis. That of the items in column (7b) is not. Stress falls on the penult, even though it is weak. The only way in

---

[8] The greater part of the analysis of the stress types is due to Alan Prince.

which the stress in column (7b) can be regularly derived is to analyze the affix as disyllabic. This disyllabic analysis is necessary only in these few cases, where both stress patterns are found.⁹

There is also a large number of contradictory cases of a different sort. In these the stress falls on the antepenult even though the penult is strong. Examples are *góvernable* and *bállastable*. This fact is in direct violation of the weak cluster principle of English stress, and there is no way to alter the phonological shape of the suffix in such a way as to allow the stress to cross the strong penult. Note, however, that the stress of the words in question is exactly that of the corresponding verbs: *govern* and *ballast*. If, therefore, we place a # boundary before the suffix, we will be able to generate the correct stress patterns in *góvernable* and *bállastable*. Similarly, and even more strikingly, words like *dísciplineable*, with initial stress, four syllables back, can be accounted for only by positing a # boundary before the suffix.

Stress facts alone thus force us to posit three suffixes. It is reasonable to believe that the disyllabic + boundary suffix is a variant of *+abl*, for the only instances in which the former occurs are those in which it varies more or less freely with the latter. No further reduction is possible and we find ourselves with two affixes: *+abl* and *#abl*.

There are minimal pairs of words, one of which contains *+abl* and the other *#abl*.

(8) a. b.
cómparable compárable
réparable repaírable
réfutable refútable
préferable preférable
dísputable dispútable

The words in column (8a) must be of the form *X+abl* and those in column (8b) of the form *X#abl*. There are semantic differences between the words in the two columns, which we will return to below.¹⁰

6.2.1.2. *Allomorphy*. The analysis accounts very nicely for the cases which involve allomorphy. We have already seen (in 5.3.2) that marked latinate roots show the same allomorphs before *-able* as they do before *-ion, -ive, -ory*, and *-or*. Curiously, however, before *-able* the allomorphy rules are optional:

(9) circumscribe circumscriptible circumscribable
extend extensible extendable
defend defensible defendable
perceive perceptible perceivable
divide divisible dividable
deride derisible deridable

⁹ Not with equal frequency. Kenyon and Knott (1953) list only *fórmidable*, but *déspicable* and *despícable, hóspitable* and *hospítable, éxplicable* and *explícable, inéxplicable* and *inexplícable* (with a note that the latter is gaining ground here).

¹⁰ We cannot account for the stress of column (8b) by claiming that the affix here is disyllabic, for then we would expect the stressed vowel to be laxed by Trisyllabic Shortening (the rule which operates on the stressed vowel of *divinity*), which it is not.

This is highly unusual; in all other instances allomorphy rules are obligatory and exceptionless. Furthermore, we do not have here a case of one or even several rules being optional before a suffix, rather the entire class of allomorphy rules seems to be optional before *-able* and only before *-able*. This is very strange, and to handle it by exception features, though feasible, would be very costly and unenlightening. The point is not that certain rules are optional, but rather that a class of rules is optional, and exception features cannot handle the notion "class of rules".

If, however, we posit two suffixes +*abl* and #*abl*, then the facts of (9) fall out immediately. The first, a + boundary suffix, can trigger allomorphy rules, while the second, a # boundary suffix, cannot. The seeming optionality of otherwise obligatory allomorphy rules is thus actually a matter of boundaries.

6.2.1.3. Truncation. As might be expected, the truncating morpheme +*At* (cf. 5.2.1 and 5.2.2) truncates before *-able*.

(10)   tolerate   tolerable
        negotiate   negotiable
        vindicate   vindicable
        demonstrate   demonstrable
        exculpate   exculpable

It is clear from the stress of words such as *demónstrable* that we are dealing here with +*abl*, not #*abl*, for if the suffix were #*abl* we would expect no stress shift between *demonstrate* and *demonstrable*, whereas if the suffix is +*abl* we expect exactly the stress pattern that we find: stress on the penult if it is strong, otherwise stress on the antepenult. Any identity in stress between the verb *Xate* and its derivative *Xable* is accidental.

Truncation of +*At* is usually obligatory. It is blocked only when there is reason for not analyzing *At* as a morpheme. So, as we noted in 5.2.2, *At* does not truncate in the word *inflatant* because to posit that *At* is a morpheme in the word *inflate* entails that the root of the word be *fl*, which is not possible, since all roots must contain a vowel. The following are similar cases:

(11)   debate   debatable   *debable
        abate   abatable   *abable
        dilate   dilatable   *dilable
        state   statable   *stable (in this sense)
        relate   relatable   *relable
        inflate   inflatable   *inflable
        translate   translatable   *translable

Truncation of +*At* is therefore either obligatory or blocked, but never optional. However, there are many cases where +*At* truncates optionally before *-able*:

(12) cultivate   cultivable   cultivatable
      educate   educable   educatable
      irrigate   irrigable   irrigatable
      navigate   navigable   navigatable
      regulate   regulable   regulatable
      frustrate   frustrable   frustratable
      filtrate   filtrable   filtratable
      demonstrate   demonstrable   demonstratable
      operate   operable   operatable
      narrate   narrable   narratable
      implicate   implicable   implicatable
      separate   separable   separatable
      allocate   allocable   allocatable
      investigate   investigable   investigatable
      anticipate   anticipable   anticipatable

This optionality can be accounted for in exactly the same way as the seeming optionality of allomorphy before *-able*, by positing the existence of the two suffixes *+abl* and *#abl*.

6.2.1.4. Summary. The phonological behavior of the suffix has been investigated, and we have found three types of evidence which strongly support the positing of two affixes, *+abl* and *#abl*. If phonology does not operate in a vacuum, then the two distinct suffixes should be differentiable on other linguistic planes as well. We will now show that they are.

6.2.2. Correlates

6.2.2.1. Morphological Correlates.[11] (a) *The Stem.* For any word containing an isolatable affix, the part of the word which consists of the whole word minus the affix in question is termed the *stem.* In words of the form *Xable*, if *X* is not an independently occurring word, then the suffix is of the form *X+abl* and not of the form *X#abl*. This is true of words which are not related to any verb, such as *possible, refrangible, vulnerable*, and *horrible*. It is also true of words which are related to a verb only through a rule of allomorphy (*divide/divisible, extend/extensible*) or truncation (*communicate/communicable, delineate/delineable*). This agrees with the theory of Siegel (1974), according to which if the stem of a word is not an independently occurring word, then the affix is always a + boundary affix.

(b) *Negative Prefixes.* The two most common negative prefixes in English are *in+* and *un#. in+* attaches to adjectives of the form *X+abl* and *un#* attaches to adjectives of the form *X#abl*.[12]

[11] Morphology is a subpart of syntax in the broad sense of that term.

[12] There are a few examples of *in+ X#abl*: *inconceivable, indescribable*. Cases of *un#X+abl* are easier to find. The reason for the imbalance in the numbers of exceptions is the difference in the productivity of *in+* and *un#*. These two prefixes, though not as strikingly minimal a pair as *+abl* and *#abl*, can be subjected to a similar comparison, as can their French counterparts: *in+* and *in#* (cf. Zimmer (1964, 50-51)).

(13) | Type | in+ | un# |
|---|---|---|
| Nonlexical stem (+abl) | impossible | *unpossible |
| | impalpable | *unpalpable |
| At+ | irregulable | *unregulable |
| | inviolable | *unviolable |
| At# | *irregulatable | unregulatable |
| | *inviolatable | unviolatable |
| Allomorphic root +abl | imperceptible | *unperceptible |
| | indivisible | *undivisible |
| Allomorphic root #abl | *imperceivable | unperceivable |
| | *individable | undividable |
| Stress differentiated +abl | irreparable | *unreparable |
| | irrevocable | *unrevocable |
| Stress differentiated #abl | *irrepairable | unrepairable |
| | *irrevokable | unrevokable |

The facts of (13) correlate perfectly with our analysis, and they serve to clear up a possible ambiguity in it. One might view +abl as a decayed #abl. On this view, which is put forth in SPE, #abl is the basic affix, and it sometimes decays to +abl. We would then have a rule such as (14) as a readjustment rule.

(14) #abl → +abl (optional, obligatory with nonlexical stems)

However, a rule such as this entails that the choice of negative prefix be made after a form has undergone a readjustment rule, i.e. in the midst of a phonological derivation.

It is also possible to think of +abl and #abl as different affixes. If we have two separate affixes, #abl and +abl, then we do not need rule (14). The fact that the choice of suffixes is sometimes optional and sometimes obligatory will be a fact about the affixes and not encoded into a rule, and the choice of suffix can be made prior to the phonology. This latter analysis seems preferable, and will receive further support from semantic facts.

6.2.2.2. Syntactic Correlates. Most words of the form *Xable* are adjectives. A very few are nouns (*tangibles, vegetables, sparables*), though all can be reified with *the*:

(15) He has just explained the inexplicable.

The *base* of any complex word is the word from which it is derived. The base is not identical to the stem. For example, the base of the word *regulable* is the word *regulate*, while its stem is *regul*, which is not a word.

Not all words of the form *X+abl* have a base. Words like *possible, probable,* and *refrangible* do not. When a word of the form *X+abl* has a base, the base is a transitive verb. The one exception I know of is *reputable*, from *repute*, a noun.

All words of the form *X#abl* have a base, which is a transitive verb.[13]

---

[13] Sometimes it is a noun: *customable, saleable*. We have already argued (in 4.1.1) that a different suffix is at work in these cases.

Ross (1974) has done extensive work on the relationship between subcategorization and lexical category. One of his discoveries is that productively derived deverbal entities are much stricter in the range of subcategorizations they enjoy than are simple verbs. Looking at verbal prefixes such as *mis#*, *re#*, and *de#*, he found that they attach to verbs with NP objects and not to verbs with particles or prepositional phrases. So, for example, we find *reinspect* but **relook at*, *misreport his income* but **misreport that he had left*.

Now, looking at the subcategorization possibilities of the two classes $X+abl$ and $X\#abl$, we find that $X+abl$ allows a prepositional phrase more frequently than $X\#abl$. Where $X+abl$ has no lexical base, prepositional phrases are common:

(16) I am amenable to a change in plans.
It's visible to the naked eye.
He's eligible for reappointment.
That's compatible with our findings.

Where we get both x_i+abl and $x_i\#abl$, and the base is a verb that allows a prepositional phrase, then the former, but not the latter, sometimes allows the prepositional phrase:

(17) divisible by three
?dividable by three
divisible into three parts
?dividable into three parts

In general, then, the subcategorization of $X\#abl$ is closer to the type isolated by Ross as characteristic of productively derived items.

6.2.2.3. Semantic Correlates. In the ideal world, the meaning of a morphologically complex word will be a compositional function of the meaning of its parts. The basic compositional meaning which has been proposed for words of the form *Xable* is 'liable to be *Y*ed' or 'capable of being *Y*ed' (where *Y* is the base of the word in question). This meaning presupposes the general case, where *Y* is a verb. Of course, when a word has no discernible base, as is the case with many words of the form $X+abl$, there is no way in which we can see whether the meaning of the whole is a function of the meaning of the parts, since the parts have no independently established meaning. This general fact has already been discussed at length in chapters 2 and 4. Therefore, the meaning of many words of the form $X+abl$ will not so much diverge from compositionality as not involve compositionality. These words apart, however, when we have two words of the form *Xable* with the same base y_i, the word of the form $Y\#abl$ will always be closer to compositionality than the word of the form $X+abl$. We will exemplify this phenomenon with several pairs:

cómparable ($X+abl$) vs. compárable ($Y\#abl$)
The meaning of *compárable* is 'capable of being compared', as in (18):

(18) The two models are simply not compárable.

One meaning of *cómparable* is that of *compárable* in (18), as can be seen by substitution:

(19) The two models are simply not cómparable.

However, *cómparable* also has another meaning, exemplified in (20), which is the same as one meaning of *equivalent*.

(20) This is the cómparable model in our line.

Compárable does not have this meaning:

(21) *This is the compárable model in our line.

tolerable (X+abl) vs. toleratable (Y#abl)

One sense of *tolerable* is 'moderately good, fair' as in (22). *Toleratable* does not have this sense, but only that of 'capable of being tolerated'.

(22) We ate a toler(*at)able lunch.

(23) How are you feeling today? Toler(*at)able.

appreciable (X+abl) vs. appreciatable (Y#abl)

Appreciable has a sense which is roughly synonymous with *substantial*:

(24) An appreciable majority favored the plan.

Appreciatable has no such sense.

perceptible (X+abl) vs. perceivable (Y#abl)

One of the meanings of *perceptible* is parallel to the sense of *appreciable* in (24) and means roughly 'large enough to matter', as in (25):

(25) There is a perceptible difference in quality.

This meaning shows up best in the negative *imperceptible*, which usually means 'insignificant', as in (26):

(26) There is a flaw in the grain, but it's imperceptible.

Perceivable does not have this meaning:

(27) *There is a flaw in the grain, but it's unperceivable.

Rather, something is perceivable if it is capable of being perceived, regardless of its size or significance. A flaw may be perceivable, even if it is not perceptible.

The reader may construct other examples. In doing so, however, note that I do not claim that words of the form X#abl never diverge from compositionality; that would be patently false. *advisable, excitable,* and *sensible* all have meanings which diverge from compositionality. The point is that when we do have pairs, then the word of the form X+abl is always the one to diverge from strict compositionality.

6.2.3. Summary. I have isolated in this section the morphological, syntactic, and semantic correlates of the difference between +abl and #abl. Morphologically, #abl has a base of the category Verb, while +abl often has no base. Syntactically, #abl adheres more closely to an archetypal pattern. Semantically, #abl is closer to compositionality. Clearly, in all these three matters, the difference between the two affixes is not one of kind, but purely one of degree. In each, there is a sense in which #*abl* is stronger, and this falls in perfectly with the phonological difference between the two. The sound and meaning of the boundaries are not arbitrarily but systematically linked. Boundaries are therefore part of linguistic structure or theory, and have no substance.

References

Anderson, S. R. (1975) "On the Interaction of Phonological Rules of Various Types," *Journal of Linguistics* 11, 39-63.

Anderson, S. R. and R. P. V. Kiparsky, eds. (1973) *A Festschrift for Morris Halle*, Holt, Rinehart and Winston, New York.

Bally, C. (1940) "Sur la motivation des signes linguistiques," *Bulletin de la Société de Linguistique de Paris* 41, 75-88.

Ben-Moshe, M. hadiqduq hane'eman, ms. CF1046, Biblioteca Ebraia, Venezia.

Bierwisch, M. (1967) "Syntactic Features in Morphology: General Problems of So-Called Pronominal Inflection in German," *To Honor Roman Jakobson*, Mouton, The Hague.

Bierwisch, M. and K. E. Heidolph, eds. (1970) *Progress in Linguistics*, Mouton, The Hague.

Binnick, R., A. Davison, G. Green, and J. Morgan, eds. (1969) *Papers from the Fifth Regional Meeting of the Chicago Linguistics Society*, Linguistics Department, University of Chicago, Chicago, Illinois.

Bloch, B. (1947) "English Verb Inflection," *Language* 23, 399-418; reprinted in M. Joos, ed. (1966).

Bloch, B. and G. Trager (1942) *Outline of Linguistic Analysis*, Special Publications of the LSA, Linguistic Society of America, Baltimore, Maryland.

Bloomfield, L. (1933) *Language*, Holt, New York.

Botha, R. P. (1968) *The Function of the Lexicon in Transformational Generative Grammar*, Mouton, The Hague.

Brame, M. (1972a) "The Segmental Cycle," in M. Brame, ed. (1972b).

Brame, M., ed. (1972b) *Contributions to Generative Phonology*, University of Texas Press, Austin, Texas.

Brame, M. (1974) "The Cycle in Phonology: Stress in Palestinian, Maltese, and Spanish," *Linguistic Inquiry* 5, 39-60.

Brown, A. F. (1958) *The Derivation of English Adjectives Ending in -ful*, unpublished Doctoral dissertation, University of Pennsylvania, Philadelphia, Pennsylvania.

Browne, E. W. (1974) "On the Topology of Anaphoric Peninsulas," *Linguistic Inquiry* 5, 619-620.

Carrier, J. (1975) "Reduplication in Tagalog," mimeographed paper, MIT, Cambridge, Massachusetts.

REFERENCES

Cena, R. M. (1975) "The Cycle Revisited: Data from Tagalog," unpublished paper, University of Alberta, Edmonton.

Chapin, P. (1967) *On the Syntax of Word-Derivation in English*, unpublished Doctoral dissertation, MIT, Cambridge, Massachusetts.

Chapin, P. (1970) "On Affixation in English," in M. Bierwisch and K. E. Heidolph, eds. (1970).

Chomsky, N. (1957) *Syntactic Structures*, Mouton, The Hague.

Chomsky, N. (1964) *Current Issues in Linguistic Theory*, Mouton, The Hague.

Chomsky N. (1965) *Aspects of the Theory of Syntax*, MIT Press, Cambridge, Massachusetts.

Chomsky, N. (1970) "Remarks on Nominalization," in R. Jacobs and P. S. Rosenbaum, eds. (1970).

Chomsky, N. (1972a) *Language and Mind*, enlarged edition, Harcourt, Brace, Jovanovich, New York.

Chomsky, N. (1972b) *Studies on Semantics in Generative Grammar*, Mouton, The Hague.

Chomsky, N. (1973) "Conditions on Transformations," in S. R. Anderson and R. P. V. Kiparsky, (1973).

Chomsky, N. and M. Halle (1968) *The Sound Pattern of English*, Harper and Row, New York.

Corum, C. (1973) "Anaphoric Peninsulas," in C. Corum et al., eds. (1973).

Corum, C., T. Smith-Stark, and A. Weiser, eds. (1973) *Papers from the Ninth Regional Meeting of the Chicago Linguistics Society*, Linguistics Department, University of Chicago, Chicago, Illinois.

Culicover, P. (1972) "OM- Sentences. On the Derivation of Sentences with Systematically Unspecified Interpretations," *Foundations of Language* 8, 199-236.

Emonds, J. (1966) "A Study of Some Very Confusing Suffixes: or Phonetic Regularities in Some Words Derived from Romance Tongues," mimeographed paper, MIT, Cambridge, Massachusetts.

Fujimura, O., ed. (1973) *Three Dimensions of Linguistic Theory*, TEC Company, Tokyo.

Gesenius F. H. W. (1962) *Hebräische Grammatik*, mit Benutzung der von E. Kautsch bearb. 28 Auflage von Wilhelm Gesenius' hebräischer Grammatik, verfasst von G. Bergsträsser. Mit Beträgen von M. Lidzbarski, G. Olm, Hildesheim.

Halle, M. (1962) "Phonology in a Generative Grammar," *Word* 18, 54-72.

Halle, M. (1973a) "Prolegomena to a Theory of Word-Formation," *Linguistic Inquiry* 4, 3-16.

Halle, M. (1973b) "The Accentuation of Russian Words," *Language* 49, 2, 312-348.

Halle, M. (1973c) "Stress Rules in English: A New Version," *Linguistic Inquiry* 4, 451-464.

Halle, M. and J. Keyser (1971) *English Stress; Its Form, Its Growth, and Its Role in Verse*, Harper and Row, New York.

Harris, Z. (1948) "Componential Analysis of a Hebrew Paradigm," *Language* 24, 87-91. Reprinted in M. Joos, ed. (1966).

Harris, Z. (1951) *Methods in Structural Linguistics*, University of Chicago Press, Chicago.

Hervey, S. G. and J. W. F. Mulder (1973) "Pseudo-Composites and Pseudo-Words: Sufficient and Necessary Criteria for Morphological Analysis," *La Linguistique* 9, No. 1, 41-70.

Hill, K. C. (1969) "Some Implications of Serrano Phonology," in R. Binnick et al., eds. (1969).

Hockett, C. F. (1947) "Problems of Morphemic Analysis," *Language* 23, 321-343. Reprinted in M. Joos, ed. (1966).

Hockett, C. F. (1958) *A Course in Modern Linguistics*, Macmillan, New York.

Horn, L. (1972) *On the Semantic Properties of Logical Operators in English*, unpublished Doctoral dissertation, UCLA, Los Angeles, California.

Householder, F. (1972) "A Problem in Rule Ordering??" *Linguistic Inquiry* 3, 392-393.

Isačenko A. V. (1972) "Rol, usečenija b russkom slovoobrazovanii," *International Journal of Slavic Linguistics and Poetics* 15, 95-125.

Jackendoff, R. S. (1972) *Semantic Interpretation in Generative Grammar*, MIT Press, Cambridge, Massachusetts.

Jackendoff, R. S. (1975) "Morphological and Semantic Regularities in the Lexicon," *Language* 51, 639-671.

Jacobs, R. and P. S. Rosenbaum, eds. (1970) *Readings in English Transformational Grammar*, Ginn, Waltham, Massachusetts.

Jepersen, O. (1954) *A Modern English Grammar on Historical Principles*, Ejnar Munksgaard, Copenhagen.

Joos, M., ed. (1966) *Readings in Linguistics I*, 4th edition, University of Chicago Press, Chicago, Illinois.

Kean, M. L. (1974) "Strict Cyclicity in Phonology," *Linguistic Inquiry* 5, 179-203.

Kenyon, J. and T. Knott (1953) *A Pronouncing Dictionary of American English*, Merriam, Springfield, Massachusetts.

Kiefer, F. (1970) *Swedish Morphology*, Swedish Institute, Stockholm.

Kiefer, F. (1973) *Generative Morphologie des Neufranzösischen*, Tübingen.

Kiparsky, P. (1966) "Uber den deutschen Akzent," *Studia Grammatica* 7.

Kiparsky, P. (1973) "Phonological Representations," in O. Fujimura, ed. (1973).

Kisseberth, C. (1972) "Cyclical Rules in Klamath Phonology," *Linguistic Inquiry* 3, 3-34.

Koerner, O. (1972) *Contributions au Débat Post-Saussurien sur le Signe Linguistique*, Mouton, The Hague.

Lees, R. B. (1960) *The Grammar of English Nominalizations* (Indiana University Research Center in Anthropology, Folklore, and Linguistics, Publication No. 12), Indiana University Press, Bloomington, Indiana.

Lightner, T. H. (1972) "Coexistent Systems in Phonology," in D. S. Worth, ed. (1972).

Marchand, H. (1969) *The Categories and Types of Present-Day English Word-Formation*, 2nd edition, Beck, München.

Martin, S. (1972) "*-ive* and Other *-ion* Based Suffixes," unpublished paper, MIT, Cambridge, Massachusetts.

Matthews, P. H. (1974) *Morphology: An Introduction to the Theory of Word-Structure*, Cambridge University Press, Cambridge.

Milligan, S., H. Secombe, and P. Sellers (1956) *Tales of Old Dartmoor*, BBC, London.

REFERENCES

Munro, P. and P. J. Benson (1973) "Reduplication and Rule Ordering in Luiseño," *IJAL* 39, 15-21.

Nida, E. A. (1948) "The Identification of Morphemes," *Language* 24, 414-441. Reprinted in M. Joos, ed. (1966).

Nida, E. A. (1949) *Morphology. The Descriptive Analysis of Words*, 2nd and completely new edition, University of Michigan Publication in Linguistics II, Ann Arbor, Michigan.

Normal and Reverse English Word List, compiled under the direction of A. F. Brown, prepared at the University of Pennsylvania under a contract with the Air Force Office of Scientific Research (AF 49 (638)-1042).

Oehrle, R. (1971) *"The Role of Morphology in the Assignment of Stress,"* unpublished paper, MIT, Cambridge, Massachusetts.

Oehrle, R. (1975) *The Grammatical Status of the English Dative Alternation*, unpublished Doctoral dissertation, MIT, Cambridge, Massachusetts.

The Oxford English Dictionary (1933), Oxford University Press, Oxford.

Peters, S., ed. (1972) *Goals of Linguistic Theory*, Prentice-Hall, Englewood Cliffs, New Jersey.

Pope, E. (1972) "Gh-words," *Linguistic Inquiry* 3, 125-130.

Postal, P. (1969) "Anaphoric Islands," in R. Binnick et al., eds. (1969).

Postal, P. (1972) "The Best Theory" in S. Peters, ed. (1972).

Prince, A. (1972) "IC," unpublished paper, MIT, Cambridge, Massachusetts.

Puhvel, J. ed. (1969) *Meaning and the Structure of Language*, University of California Press, Berkeley and Los Angeles, California.

Ross, J. R. (1972) "A Reanalysis of English Stress," in M. Brame, ed. (1972b).

Ross, J. R. (1973) "Leftward Ho!" in S. R. Anderson and P. Kiparsky, eds. (1973).

Ross, J. R. (1974) "Wording Up," lectures presented at the Linguistic Institute, University of Massachusetts, Amherst, Massachusetts.

de Saussure, F. (1949) *Cours de linguistique générale*, 4th edition, Payot, Paris.

Schachter, P. (1962) Review of Lees (1960), in *IJAL* 28, 134-149.

Schachter, P. and V. Fromkin (1968) *A Phonology of Akan: Akuapem, Asante, and Fante*, Working Papers in Phonetics 9, UCLA, Los Angeles, California.

Schane, S. (1968) *French Phonology and Morphology*, MIT Press, Cambridge, Massachusetts.

Schnitzer, M. (1971) "A Problem in Rule Ordering," *Linguistic Inquiry* 2, 422.

Selkirk, E. (1972) *The Phrase Phonology of English and French*, unpublished Doctoral dissertation, MIT, Cambridge, Massachusetts.

Shelvador, C. (1974) "The Semantics of + and #," *Glossolalia* 16, 415-436.

Siegel, D. (1971) "Some Lexical Transderivational Constraints in English," unpublished paper, MIT, Cambridge, Massachusetts.

Siegel, D. (1974) *Topics in English Morphology*, unpublished Doctoral dissertation, MIT, Cambridge, Massachusetts.

Spang-Hannsen, H. (1954) *Recent Theories on the Nature of the Language Sign*, (TCLC 9), Nordisk Sprog-og Kulturforlag, Copenhagen.

Stanley, R. (1967) "Redundancy Rules in Phonology," *Language* 43, 393-437.

Stanley, R. (1973) "Boundaries in Phonology," in S. R. Anderson and P. Kiparsky, eds. (1973).

Stevens, A. (1968) *Madurese Phonology and Morphology*, American Oriental Series 52, American Oriental Society, New Haven, Connecticut.

Ullmann, S. (1957) *The Principles of Semantics*, second edition, Philosophical Library, New York.

Ullmann, S. (1962) *Semantics, An Introduction to the Science of Meaning*, Blackwell, Oxford.

Vergnaud, J. R. (1973) "Formal Properties of Lexical Derivations," *Quarterly Progress Report of the Research Laboratory of Electronics*, No. 108, MIT, Cambridge, Massachusetts.

Vergnaud, J. R. (1974) *French Relative Clauses*, unpublished Doctoral dissertation, MIT, Cambridge, Massachusetts.

Walker, J. (1936) *Walker's Rhyming Dictionary*, revised and enlarged by L. H. Dawson, Dutton, New York.

Webster's Third New International Dictionary (1971), Merriam, Springfield, Massachusetts.

Weinreich, U. (1969) "Problems in the Analysis of Idioms," in J. Puhvel, ed. (1969).

Wilbur, R. (1973) *The Phonology of Reduplication*, Indiana University Linguistics Club, Indiana University, Bloomington, Indiana.

Williams, E. S. (1973) "*re and back*," unpublished paper, MIT, Cambridge, Massachusetts.

Williams, E. S. (1974) *Rule Ordering in Syntax*, unpublished Doctoral dissertation, MIT, Cambridge, Massachusetts.

Wittgenstein, L. (1953) *Philosophical Investigations*, translated by G. E. M. Anscombe, Blackwell, Oxford.

Worth, D. S., ed. (1972) *The Slavic Word*, Mouton, The Hague.

Wurzel, W. (1970) *Studien zur deutschen Lautstruktur*, Akademie-Verlag, Berlin.

Zimmer, K. (1964) *Affixal Negation in English and Other Languages: An Investigation of Restricted Productivity*, supplement to *Word*, Monograph 5, New York.